APPROACHES
TO THE INFORMAL
EVALUATION
OF READING

Editors

John J. Pikulski
University of Delaware

Timothy Shanahan
University of Illinois at Chicago Circle

INTERNATIONAL READING ASSOCIATION

800 Barksdale Road   Newark, Delaware 19711

WITHDRAWN

INTERNATIONAL READING ASSOCIATION

Copyright 1982 by the
International Reading Association

Library of Congress Catologing in Publication Data
Main entry under title:

Approaches to the informal evaluation of reading.

   Bibliography: p.
   1. Reading—Ability testing.   I. Pikulski, John J.   II. Shanahan, Timothy.
LB1050.46.A66   428.4'076   81-18643
ISBN 0-87207-528-1   AACR2

Contents

Foreword

What useful information is there in a standardized test given to children all over the country in 30-45 minute sessions that a skilled teacher does not know from interacting with a group of pupils six hours a day 180 days a year? Not very much, many people feel.

The insightful teacher engages in continuous informal evaluation as this teacher-pupil interaction takes place. Much of this evaluation becomes a part of the teaching itself, a continuous kid-watching as teachers observe their pupils reading and responding to instruction. Some of it utilizes self-constructed devices or published ones for observing and analyzing what pupils are doing. These devices and procedures vary considerably in their complexity, but all of them come under the classification in this volume of informal evaluation. They are informal in contrast to formal standardized or criterion-referenced assessment tests. Beyond that they obviously vary in just how formal or informal they are. They also vary in terms of how much knowledge they require of the teacher and how much control of the process of evaluation they leave to the teacher.

Informal evaluation is done for a variety of purposes: to plan instruction, to place pupils at instructional levels, to evaluate progress, to see strengths and weaknesses.

This book brings together a group of scholars who clearly know their informal reading evaluation. They present a considerable range of such procedures; enough to extend the teacher already committed to informal evaluation, enough to inform those ready to begin informal evaluation, enough to provide an important source of information for scholars in the field.

The International Reading Association is proud to offer this important contribution to reading evaluation.

Kenneth S. Goodman, *President*
International Reading Association
1981-1982

Introduction

It is not uncommon to meet teachers who feel very insecure about testing or evaluating reading skills. Often they feel that the results obtained on a group test of reading or on some brief individual measure are inaccurate, but they feel powerless to challenge these results. This volume represents a bringing together of a large number of alternatives that can be used by such teachers. None of the papers is suggesting use of a specific test; instead they describe, in detail, procedures that teachers can use flexibly and with a wide variety of materials to answer questions that will be helpful in planning a reading instructional program for a child or group of children. These various approaches and techniques are all classified by the authors of this volume as "informal evaluation procedures."

Virtually every comprehensive treatment of the measurement of reading skills makes mention of "informal" approaches to evaluation. Like so many terms in the field of reading education, there are widely differing views of what informal reading evaluation really is. This volume takes the position that the term "informal evaluation" as applied to reading is a very broad one. Johns, in the introductory paper, outlines the many purposes for which informal measures may be used and briefly describes the various forms that informal evaluation tools may take. Cunningham looks at what ultimately may be the most powerful informal evaluation tool—teacher observation. She particularly addresses two central testing concepts, reliability and validity, that are all too often avoided in discussions for informal reading evaluation. She offers convincing argument as to why the ongoing observation that teachers can make, as they interact with pupils in an instructional setting, may be the most reliable and valid approach that one can take in the diagnosis of reading behavior.

The next five papers in the volume are somewhat more specific in purpose and scope. Botel, clearly operating from a theoretical framework that views reading as part of a larger language communication process, translates theoretical perspective and experimental results into specific suggestions for evaluating decoding as well as comprehension. Hammond specifically addresses the manner in which oral reading should be evaluated and how measures of oral reading should be interpreted. He too begins with a theoretical position and moves to practical suggestions. He looks at informal evaluation from the perspective of a psycholinguistic view of the reading process and integrates the results of the research done in the area of miscue analysis.

The paper by Pikulski and Tobin, which reviews the various forms that cloze techniques can take, illustrates the breadth of the procedures that the authors of this volume see as falling under the heading "informal evaluation." Directions offered for the construction and interpretation of cloze tests are specific enough to serve as a useful guide to reading specialists and classroom teachers interested in using this technique.

Hansell's paper offers suggestions as to how teachers in content areas can employ a variety of informal evaluation procedures to obtain information that will allow them to determine the factors that may be limiting their students from obtaining information through printed materials. All too often informal evaluation is seen as a technique appropriate only for the specially trained teacher of reading; Hansell shows that it can be profitably and efficiently used by any teacher.

Though the points of view expressed and the specific recommendations made in the various papers are not always in agreement, a thread that runs through all of this is that reading must be viewed as a linguistic process and as part of the larger area of language and communication. Cramer specifically illustrates the interrelatedness of the language skills by suggesting that if teachers begin to diagnostically analyze the writing that students produce, they will gain many insights into general language skills and more specifically into the reading skills that the students possess.

The final paper is somewhat different from the others because rather than offering suggestions for the administration and interpretation of reading diagnostic procedures, it reviews the evidence that exists regarding the values and limitations of a specfic form of testing—Informal Reading Inventories (IRIs). Unlike the point of view taken in this volume, there are many who would equate informal evaluation with IRIs, and, indeed, IRIs remain one of the most common forms of reading evaluation used. Pikulski and Shanahan review the research that addresses questions surrounding the use of these very popular instruments.

In addition to the common thread of viewing reading as being part of the language process, the papers in this volume have at least one other quality—they are nondogmatic. They consistently make modest claims for the techniques being recommended; they consistently suggest that the results of any reading evaluation must be viewed as tentative; they also consistently suggest that unless the results are carefully, critically interpreted by informed, capable reading specialists in the larger framework of a student's day-to-day reading performance, the results of an evaluation will be useless, and in some cases, potentially destructive.

JJP

TS

The International Reading Association attempts, through its publications, to provide a
forum for a wide spectrum of opinions on reading. This policy permits divergent
viewpoints without assuming the endorsement of the Association.

The Dimensions and Uses of Informal Reading Assessment

Jerry L. Johns
Northern Illinois University

Purposes for Evaluation

The uses of informal evaluation vary considerably. While one teacher might construct an informal reading test to assess a student's ability to use maps in a social studies book, another teacher might use students' performances on workbook pages to help assess their ability to use context cues or other reading strategies. This article provides an overview of selected informal strategies for assessing reading and reading-related behavior. A perspective on informal assessment is given, followed by descriptions and examples of the major types of informal assessment strategies.

Perspective on Informal Assessment in Reading

Informal tests and measures of reading performance vary widely in their scope and sophistication. They also vary widely in their validity and reliability which tend to depend, to a large degree, on the care given to their construction and the uses for which they are employed.

Any type of assessment in reading must begin with clearly defined purposes. There are at least four major purposes for informal assessment: 1) studying, evaluating, or diagnosing reading behavior; 2) monitoring student progress; 3) supplementing and confirming information gained from standardized and criterion-referenced instruments; and 4) obtaining information not readily available from other sources.

Informal Reading Assessment

As teachers develop, select, or use informal assessment strategies, it is important that they keep their purposes in mind. Teachers need to know whether their assessment focus is on schools, classrooms, individuals, lessons, or programs. The range of grades or areas of assessment should also be considered. Generally, teachers tend to concern themselves with aspects of their program of reading instruction, which implies that the assessment strategies will be designed to assess students in a classroom setting. There are also various levels of assessment. The *survey* level focuses on global skills and abilities. The *specific* level focuses on a particular skill or ability. The *intensive* level concerns an in-depth appraisal of a student's reading behavior and is often accomplished by a specialist in a clinic or remedial setting.

Major Types of Informal Assessment Strategies

The inner-ocular technique. For years teachers have been using what this author has chosen to call the inner-ocular technique (IOT) for assessing and monitoring the reading program (Johns, 1979a). The term was invented in hopes that this pseudo-scientific abbreviation might help teachers legitimize something they have always done: use observation skills to help determine whether their instruction is producing the desired results. This form of evaluation is what Cunningham has referred to in this volume as "diagnosis by observation." Careful and systematic observation can help teachers place students in appropriate materials; assess readiness for a given task; determine reading interest; assess attitudes; and make decisions about decoding, comprehension, and study skills. When teachers put their observation skills to work, they employ a powerful form of assessment. Perhaps one of the most compelling reasons for using the IOT is that it provides a continuous method to monitor or evaluate the student's successes and failures in important components of the reading program. The IOT is a dynamic process that builds on day-to-day behavior. A detailed discussion of the value and forms that this type of assessment takes is included in the next chapter of this volume.

Conferences. Related to the IOT is the teacher-student conference. Such conferences, while brief, can help the teacher become better acquainted with the student, assess attitudes toward reading, uncover strategies for reconstructing meaning from print, explore possible interests, discuss the book the student is reading, assess oral reading (note that round-robin oral reading is not used), and explore the student's notions about reading.

Conferences can frequently be strengthened by making notes after the conference or using a checklist of items frequently discussed. Notecards, folders, or notebooks have been used successfully by teachers to keep records. Hill (1979) has provided an extensive set of questions that can be used with older students during conferences to assess their reading-study habits.

Informal reading inventory. Perhaps the most widely known form of systematic informal assessment is the informal reading inventory (IRI). An IRI is an individually administered reading test composed of a series of graded word lists and graded passages that the student reads aloud to the teacher. As the student reads, the teacher notes oral reading errors or miscues such as mispronunciations, omissions, repetitions, and substitutions. After the oral reading, the teacher asks the student comprehension questions. Silent reading passages and passages read to the student to determine a listening comprehension level, both accompanied by comprehension checks, are also usually included.

The student's performance on the IRI forms the basis for establishing a student's independent, instructional, and frustration reading levels as well as strengths and weaknesses in word recognition and comprehension. Perhaps the most important use of the IRI is to help the teacher match the student's reading ability with appropriate instructional materials. Some educators believe that as many as 50 to 70 percent of students are placed in books that are too difficult. Matching students with the appropriate difficulty level of reading materials, therefore, may be one of the most important actions a teacher can take to improve instruction.

In addition to determining the proper level for instruction, teachers can also use the results of an IRI to better understand the student's word attack and comprehension strategies. Areas frequently evaluated include context and language cues, phonic cues, structural analysis, and the ability to answer various types of comprehension questions. Once the student's strengths and weaknesses have been determined, appropriate reading strategy lessons may be developed. The following sources provide guidelines for the preparation of strategy lessons: Allen and Watson (1976), Christie (1979), Gillespie-Silver (1979), Johns (1975), Maring (1978), and Spiegel (1978).

Teachers may either construct their own IRIs or purchase commercially published inventories. In 1977, Johns and others prepared a list of published reading inventories. Some of the IRIs that have been published since 1977 include the following:

Analytical reading inventory, 2nd ed. (primer through 9). Charles E. Merrill Publishing, 1300 Alum Creek Drive, Columbus, Ohio 43216.

Advanced reading inventory (grades 7 through college). William C. Brown Company, 2460 Kerper Boulevard, Dubuque, Iowa 52001.

Basic reading inventory, 2nd ed. (preprimer through 8). Kendall/Hunt Publishing, 2460 Kerper Boulevard, Dubuque, Iowa 52001.

Ekwall reading inventory (preprimer through 9). Allyn and Bacon, 470 Atlantic Avenue, Boston, Massachusetts 02210.

Informal reading assessment (preprimer through 12). Rand McNally, Box 7600, Chicago, Illinois 60680.

For those who are interested in preparing their own IRIs, the following sources are recommended: Johnson and Kress (1965), Leibert (1969), Valmont (1972), and Zintz (1975). Research related to the effectiveness of informal reading inventories is summarized in this volume in the chapter by Pikulski and Shanahan.

Cloze procedure. The cloze procedure is yet another form of informal evaluation that can be used for a variety of assessment purposes. Generally, it involves omitting words from paragraphs of material, replacing the omitted word with blanks of uniform length, and asking students to fill in the omitted words.

Teachers who wish to use the cloze procedure for evaluating the suitability of reading materials should refer to the chapter in this volume by Pikulski and Tobin. It includes details related to constructing, scoring, and interpreting cloze tests.

Teachers can use cloze informally to help teach students how to use context cues and to improve their comprehension

(Jongsma, 1980). The general procedure is to delete words in some rational manner; e.g., verbs or nouns. Students are then told to fill in a word that makes sense. After words have been supplied, a discussion of the appropriateness of students' responses occurs. When cloze is used to teach context cues or to improve comprehension, synonym scoring of responses is recommended. Teachers can ask students whether the word(s) they suggest make sense in the context of the sentence, paragraph, or passage.

Teachers may find the work of Rankin (1977) particularly helpful in developing strategies for introducing the cloze procedure, selecting reading passages and word deletions, using visual cues, and providing appropriate reinforcements. An annotated bibliography on the cloze procedure has been prepared by McKenna and Robinson (1980). Other recent sources for helping teachers use the cloze procedure include Arnold and Miller (1980) and Ekwall (1976).

Attitude inventories. More and more teachers realize that a reading program, if it is to be successful, must have at least two major goals: to teach students how to read, and to create students who *want* to read. Measurements of students' attitudes become important if the second goal of the reading program is to be achieved.

Attitude surveys represent one way of obtaining some notion of students' attitudes toward reading. In the primary grades, statements like the following could be read to students who could respond by circling yes/no on an answer sheet or circling the appropriate face (☺ ☹).

> I can read as fast as the good readers.
> I like to read.
> I like to read long stories.
> The books I read in school are too hard.
> I need more help in reading.
> I worry quite a bit about my reading in school.
> I read at home.
> I would rather read than watch television.
> I am a poor reader.
> I like my parents to read to me.

In the middle grades, students could respond to the following ten statements by circling agree, undecided, or disagree on their answer sheets:

Reading is a good way to spend spare time.
Most books are too long and dull.
There should be more free reading in school.
Reading is as important as watching television.
Reading is boring.
Reading is rewarding to me.
I think reading is fun.
Teachers ask me to read books that are too hard.
I am a poor reader.
My parents spend quite a bit of time reading.

There are several questionnaires that have been published to help measure students' attitudes toward reading. Questionnaires that may be of interest to teachers include:

Askov, Eunice N. *Primary pupil reading attitude inventory.* Dubuque, Iowa: Kendall/Hunt, 1973.

Estes, Thomas E. A scale to measure attitudes toward reading, *Journal of Reading,* November 1971, *15,* 135-138. Further validation of this scale can be found in Kenneth L. Dulin and Robert D. Chester, A validation study of the Estes attitude scale, *Journal of Reading,* October 1974, *18,* 56-59.

Heathington, Betty S., and Alexander, J. Estill. A child-based observation checklist to assess attitudes toward reading. *Reading Teacher,* April 1978, *31,* 769-771.

LaPray, Margaret. *Helping children to become independent readers.* New York: Center for Applied Research in Education, 1972.

Rowell, C. Glennon. An attitude scale for reading. *Reading Teacher,* February 1972, *25,* 442-447.

Tullock-Rhody, Regina, and Alexander, J. Estill. A scale for assessing attitudes toward reading in secondary schools. *Journal of Reading,* April 1980, *23,* 609-614.

Vaughan, Joseph L. Jr. A scale to measure attitudes toward teaching reading in content classrooms. *Journal of Reading,* April 1977, *20,* 605-609.

Johns

Interest inventories. Most interest inventories consist of a series of questions or incomplete sentences that help teachers find out such things as students' likes, dislikes, hobbies, interests, family activities, and use of free time. The inventories can be administered orally or in written form. One of the major reasons for administering an interest inventory is to gain information to help use instructional techniques and books appropriate to students' interests and needs.

One informal student interest inventory is in the form of a news story. Incomplete sentences help students write about their family, friends, pets, wishes, travels, hobbies, television, and books. Several sample incomplete sentences include:

My father and I like to _____.
I would like to have a pet _____.
I do not like _____.
My _____ reads to me.
One of my hobbies is _____.

In addition, some of the following questions may be useful:
What kinds of books or stories do you like?
What books or magazines do you have at home?
Which comic books do you like to read?

Numerous interest inventories are available for use or adaptation by teachers in the following sources:

Farr, Roger, and Roser, Nancy. *Teaching a child to read.* New York: Harcourt Brace Jovanovich, 1979.

Harris, Larry A., and Smith, Carl B. *Reading instruction,* 3rd ed. New York: Holt, Rinehart and Winston, 1980.

Strickler, Darryl, and Eller, William. Attitudes and interests. In Pose Lamb and Richard Arnold (Eds.), *Teaching Reading.* Belmont, California: Wadsworth, 1980.

After the student has completed an inventory, the teacher can review and study the responses to get clues about interest patterns. Because interest and reading preferences are largely individual and subject to change, teachers should use caution in drawing conclusions.

Workbooks and worksheets. The many worksheets and workbook pages included in most reading programs provide another means for assessing reading skills on a regular basis. The workbook pages and worksheets are designed to provide practice with a particular reading skill, such as selecting the main idea of a short passage. If that worksheet is composed of a series of short passages and several statements (one of which is the main idea), the teacher can use the exercise as one method to determine which students may need additional instruction with the skill of identifying main ideas.

An advantage of worksheets and workbook pages is their accessibility. Carefully selecting appropriate workbook or worksheet exercises will provide the teacher with an ongoing means of assessment that, if properly used, can help evaluate the effectiveness of skills instruction.

Other informal measures. There are several additional informal means of gathering information to aid in assessing reading: cumulative records, student-kept records, and numerous other informal tests.

Cumulative records are one means for developing a longitudinal view of the student's reading. Such records usually contain test results (standardized and informal), observations by previous teachers, health and family information, attendance records, books read, and special instruction that has been given. Although cumulative records sometimes contain vague and somewhat subjective materials, they can sometimes provide insight for instruction or suggest an interest area that can be used to motivate the student's reading.

Student-kept records can be initiated by teachers to help the student keep track of books read, favorite stories, scores on workbooks/worksheets, or progress in various learning centers. These records may provide insights into numerous areas of the reading program.

There are a host of informal tests that the teacher can construct to assess prereading, decoding, and comprehension skills. Some of these informal tests require little effort to construct while others demand several hours. For example, a teacher who wishes to determine which students may need instruction in the thirteen most common basic sight words (Johns, 1979b) could merely prepare a card containing the words (a, and, for, he, in, is, it, of, that, the, to, was, you). As the student says the words, the teacher records responses on a simple record sheet.

In the upper grades, informal tests of study skills and the ability to use the textbooks are sometimes constructed by teachers. Teachers in the upper grades may find the following sources useful for constructing informal tests that help evaluate whether students can profit from and effectively use content area materials.

Karlin, Robert. *Teaching reading in high school,* 3rd ed. Indianapolis: Bobbs-Merrill, 1977.

Viox, Ruth G. *Evaluating reading and study skills in the secondary classroom: A guide for content teachers.* Newark, Delaware: International Reading Association, 1968.

Summary

Various informal techniques have been described to help teachers assess students' reading behavior. No single method of assessment is sufficiently valid or reliable that it alone should form the basis of assessment.

Teachers need to realize that informal tests represent one part of a balanced assessment program. Standardized, diagnostic, and criterion-referenced tests should also be used.

TYPES AND AREAS OF INFORMAL ASSESSMENT

Type of Informal Assessment	Areas of Assessment						
	Placement	Prereading	Decoding	Comprehension	Study Skills	Personal Reading	Interest/ Attitudes
Inner-Ocular Technique	x	x	x	x	x	x	x
Conferences	x	x	x	x	x	x	x
Informal Reading Inventory	x		x	x			x
Cloze Procedure	x			x			
Attitude Inventories						x	x
Interest Inventories						x	x
Workbook/Worksheets		x	x	x	x		

Without this balance, instruction may become misdirected, which, in turn, may work against helping students become efficient and effective readers. All teachers use some of these informal techniques. Teachers need to remember that informal assessment techniques are a legitimate means to gain insights into the teaching of reading.

To help teachers use the informal strategies described in this article, the chart on page 9 may be useful in showing some of the major areas in the reading program that may be evaluated with informal measures.

References

Allen, P. David, & Watson, Dorothy J. (Eds.). *Findings of research in miscue analysis: Classroom implications.* Urbana, Illinois: National Council of Teachers of English, 1976.

Arnold, Richard, & Miller, John. Word recognition skills. In Pose Lamb & Richard Arnold (Eds.), *Teaching reading: Foundations and strategies,* 2nd ed. Belmont, California: Wadsworth, 1980.

Christie, James F. The qualitative anaylsis system: Updating the IRI, *Reading World,* 1979, *18,* 393-399.

Ekwall, Eldon E. *Diagnosis and remediation of the disabled reader.* Boston: Allyn and Bacon, 1976.

Gillespie-Silver, Patricia. *Teaching reading to children with special needs.* Columbus, Ohio: Charles E. Merrill, 1979.

Hill, Walter R. *Secondary school reading: Process, program, procedure.* Boston: Allyn and Bacon, 1979.

Johns, Jerry L. Reading assessment: The third dimension. *Reading Horizons,* 1979 (a), *19,* 235-236.

Johns, Jerry L. Strategies for oral reading behavior. *Language Arts,* 1975, *52,* 1104-1107.

Johns, Jerry L. Vocabulary: Perspectives and teaching strategies. In Kenneth VanderMeulen (Ed.), *Reading horizons: Selected readings.* Kalamazoo, Michigan: Western Michigan University Press, 1979 (b).

Johns, Jerry L., Garton, Sharon, Schoenfelder, Paula, & Skriba, Patricia (Compilers). *Assessing reading behavior: Informal reading inventories.* Newark, Delaware: International Reading Association, 1977.

Johnson, Marjorie Seddon, & Kress, Roy A. *Informal reading inventories.* Newark, Delaware: International Reading Association, 1965.

Jongsma, Eugene. *Cloze instruction research: A second look.* Newark, Delaware: International Reading Association, 1980.

Leibert, Robert E. The development of informal tests of reading and the analysis of the reading performance of adults attending basic education classes. September 1969. ED 034 963

Maring, Gerald H. Matching remediation to miscues. *Reading Teacher,* 1978, *31,* 887-891.

McKenna, Michael C., & Robinson, Richard D. (Compilers). *An introduction to the cloze procedure.* Newark, Delaware: International Reading Association, 1980.

Rankin, Earl F. Sequence strategies for teaching reading comprehension with the cloze procedure. In P. David Pearson & Jane Hansen (Eds.), *Reading: Theory, research, and practice.* Twenty-Sixth Yearbook of the National Reading Conference. Clemson, South Carolina: National Reading Conference, 1977.

Spiegel, Dixie Lee. Meaning-seeking strategies for the beginning reader. *Reading Teacher,* 1978, *31,* 772-776.

Valmont, William J. Creating questions for informal reading inventories. *Reading Teacher,* 1972, *25,* 509-512.

Zintz, Miles V. *The reading process: The teacher and the learner,* 2nd ed. Dubuque, Iowa: William C. Brown, 1975.

Diagnosis by Observation

Patricia Cunningham
Wake Forest University

"Good morning, Ms. Jones. This is Johnny. Johnny just moved into our school district and he is going to be in your third grade." The principal smiles and exits leaving Johnny with Ms. Jones. Ms. Jones puts an arm around a frightened Johnny and leads him into the classroom. She appoints two of her more capable, congenial students to be Johnny's special friends for the week and makes a special effort to ensure that Johnny becomes a part of the classroom as soon as possible. Meanwhile, Ms. Jones wonders about Johnny. "On what level does he read and in which group should he be placed?" "What skills has he mastered and on which ones does he currently need to work?" "Is he a child who can identify words better than he can comprehend what he is reading, or is he a child who has trouble identifying words but makes good use of those words he can identify?"

These and many other questions go through Ms. Jones' mind as she watches Johnny become acclimated to her classroom. How will she answer these questions? Perhaps there will be some useful information in the records that will come from his old school. She may be able to gain additional information by giving Johnny some standardized or teacher-made tests. The answers to most of Ms. Jones' questions, however, will not magically appear as numbers on a score report or as right and wrong answers on a test. The answers to most of her questions will appear as Ms. Jones interacts with and systematically observes Johnny on a day-to-day basis. This system of diagnosis is sometimes labeled in reading textbooks as "diagnosis by observation." Teachers refer to it differently. "I don't know how I do it," replies a particularly effective teacher when asked how he knows which children need what when. "I just follow my intuitions," replies another teacher. "Doing what comes naturally," says a third teacher.

Good teachers know the reading needs of their students. The problem is that teachers often are unable to articulate how they know and, consequently, are unable to share their talents with others. I know this is true because, for many years, I was one of those teachers who "had a feel for what to do" and was at a loss to communicate this feeling to my principal, supervisor, or other interested teachers. For the most part, principals and supervisors, seeing that I achieved good results with children, left me alone to do it in whatever mysterious way I could. Today, however, I don't believe I would be granted that freedom. Intuition is out. Criterion referenced tests, behavioral objectives, and management skills systems are in. The implementation of these "grand plans for reading success" was probably well intentioned. There are teachers who lack "intuition" and a feel for what to do next. These teachers simply could not provide each child with appropriate instruction because they didn't know what to do. So, pencil and paper tests were designed and keyed to objectives and materials. "Intuition" would no longer be a requisite for good instruction. One need only administer and score the tests, prescribe the appropriately keyed lessons and administer some more tests. This test, prescribe, test, prescribe, sequence could then be continued over and over again. Unfortunately, these grand plans have not worked out as well in practice as one might have expected them to. While they seemed to provide a workable system for the teacher who did not know how to use observation effectively, the system was far from foolproof. When a child seemed to have mastered skills, and still wasn't learning to read, the naive teacher still didn't know what to do even when test results were available. Worse, however, was the damage done to the teaching of the intuitive teachers. Unable to explain how what they were doing worked, intuitive teachers often felt forced to adopt systems which seemed objective and precise but which often proved to be less effective and time consuming.

Occasionally, I have voiced my concerns to some of my colleagues who are advocates of skills management systems. Their

Diagnosis by Observation

responses often are that they share my concern that the intuitive teacher is being stifled and they know that no system, even the one they are advocating, is foolproof; however, they also maintain it is unreasonable to expect them to accept an "intuitive" system that can't even be explained. Although some teachers can "just do it," others can't. Can this latter group be taught to "do it?" The remainder of this article will be devoted to accepting the challenge of explaining intuitive teaching, which can also be called "diagnosis by observation."

Reliability and Validity of Diagnosis by Observation

When a test maker or a curriculum specialist attempts to sell a test to teachers or administrators, the terms validity and reliability are sure to be bandied about. Often, these technical sounding terms are accompanied by some impressive sounding numbers. "This test has clearly established concurrent validity and a test-retest reliability of .88," is the kind of argument intuitive teachers find hard to refute. Assessment must, indeed, be valid and reliable if it is going to help us make instructional decisions. Intuitive teachers have a knack for making their observations valid and reliable even though they seldom use these terms, often cannot define them, and never have impressive numbers.

A person is said to be reliable if that person can be depended on, time and time again, to do whatever he or she is expected to do. Nunnally (1967) states that, "Reliability concerns the extent to which measurements are *repeatable* by the same individual using different measures of the same attribute or by different persons using the same measure of an attribute." An assessment measure is said to be reliable if it can be depended on, time and time again, to do what it is expected to do. If a measure is very reliable, it will yield approximately the same results today as it will tomorrow or next week. You can rely on the consistency of the response. Test makers achieve reliability in a number of ways, one of which is by including many different items to measure each skill. A student may miss one of the items due to confusion, inattention, or fatigue and get most of the other items correct. Another student may correctly guess the answer to an item but show the true deficiency by responding incorrectly to the remainder of the items. The scores of both students will be fairly reliable if there are a number of different items testing the same skill because the judgment is not likely to be made based on the one chance mistake or guess.

The intuitive teacher achieves reliability in a similar manner. Judgments are never made based on one observation. When I taught first grade, we played the "whisper game" every day to conclude our reading group. I would present some task to the students: "Today, I want you each to whisper in my ear a word that begins with the letter *m*." "This morning, I have a magic sentence on my magic slate for all my good readers to whisper to me." "Whisper to me something funny that happened in today's story." The task related to a skill I was working on and, as each child finished whispering, I would unobtrusively note the success or failure on a checklist. I would never decide that a particular child knew the sound/letter correspondence for the initial consonant *m* or could read new words in context or remember major events from a story based on one day's whispering. Rather, I would repeat the tasks related to a particular skill several times. I would eventually conclude that those children who responded correctly to my task each time, or who only responded incorrectly once, were doing well with the skill in question. Children who almost never responded correctly were identified and given additional individual instruction. For the few children whose performance was inconsistent from one day to another, I would sit down with each individually and probe in more depth their understanding or lack of understanding of the skill in question.

There are many other strategies besides the whisper game by which intuitive teachers achieve the goal of reliability. All of these strategies call for making several observations of each desired skill before making a decision. Intuitive teachers use every pupil response for activities to increase student participation and to "get a feel for" which students are learning, which aren't, and which need some one-on-one probing. Intuitive teachers ask students to write down an individual response to a thought provoking question and take that written response to a small group which will discuss and perhaps even argue over the varied responses. As the children interact in small groups, the intuitive teacher is circulating and making notes about the higher level thinking abilities of each student. Intuitive teachers who have a long drive to and from school sometimes tape the oral reading of some of their children and then listen to these tapes while driving to or from school.

These and numerous other structured, planned, systematic observations carried out by intuitive teachers allow these teachers to make instructional decisions upon which they can rely. Because these observations are carried out across several days or weeks or months, the judgments achieve a high degree of reliability. Unlike judgments based on a test which is given in a single sitting, ongoing teacher observations are not affected by day-to-day changes in students' physical health or emotional stability.

The concept of validity is somewhat harder to explain than the concept of reliability. Nunnally (1967) states that, "In a very general sense, a measuring instrument is valid if it does what it is intended to do." Validity of measurement refers to the match between the concept or skill to be measured and the means by which it is measured. A measure is valid to the extent that it measures what it was intended to measure. This distinction may seem academic and superfluous since we ought to be able to assume that any instrument will measure what it is intended to measure. This assumption, however, is often questionable when one considers the limitations of pencil and paper tests. An example should clarify these limitations.

Imagine, for example, that a reading skill important for beginning readers to master is the association between consonant letters and the sounds commonly associated with these letters. Creating a valid paper and pencil test of this knowledge would appear quite simple. One could create a test which contained some pictures and ask students to write the letter they thought the name of the picture began with. Is this a valid measure of their knowledge? When the tests have been scored, will the teacher know which students have this initial consonant knowledge and which don't? The answer is, "Perhaps!" Imagine, for example, that some students don't know or can't remember the names for some of the pictures. Students who look at a picture of a dog, call it a puppy, and write the letter *p* under the picture have the wrong answer and the right knowledge. Imagine other children who write the letter *b* under the picture thinking they have the knowledge that the test was designed to evaluate. Other students may be able to spell dog, and write the letter *d* under the picture.

If this response was generated by a memorized spelling, the correct response does not indicate that the children have achieved the desired sound/symbol correspondence. In order to create a valid test of students' consonant sound knowledge, the test creator would have to be sure that most of the stimulus pictures were familiar to the children, called by the desired name, and not familiar enough to have their spelling memorized.

There is, however, a much more serious and insurmountable obstacle to the test procedure described above. This is related to the issue of why it is desirable for students to be able to associate consonant letters with sounds. This knowledge, in and of itself, is useless. It becomes useful only when the student can *use* this knowledge and the context of what is being read to decode an unfamiliar word. What we really want students to do is to *apply* their knowledge of letter/sound relationships as they read. The previously described test procedure is aimed at testing the student's letter/sound association knowledge, not the application of this in real reading. So, if the desired skill is the ability to use this knowledge in reading, how can this be measured validly? The answer to this question is obvious and simple. Put the children in a "real" reading situation in which they can demonstrate their ability.

Imagine that Mr. Jones, Master Intuitive Teacher, desires to know which students have learned consonant letter/sound associations and can apply them as they are reading. How would he find this out? He would probably carry out a lesson that looked like this:

"Boys and girls, this morning I put some sentences on the board. While I wasn't looking, a leprechaun sneaked in and covered up some of my words with these shamrocks. He must want us to play a guessing game since this is St. Patrick's Day, a special day for leprechauns. Let's read each sentence together saying 'blank' when we come to the covered words. Then let's guess which word the leprechaun covered up." (Students read the first sentence and make four or five guesses for the blank.) "We certainly have a lot of guesses. How can we decide which is right? Yes, we could uncover the whole word, but look here, the shamrocks are cut so that the left corner of each comes off. The leprechaun must want us to have some extra clues. Let's tear just this corner off." (Corner is torn off revealing the initial consonant of the word.) "Aha! He did give us some extra clues. Now, which of our guesses are still possible? Yes, that word begins with an *l* so it could be lake but not pond, ocean, or river. Let's try the rest in the same way. First, without any clues we will guess how the word begins. Then, we will make new guesses based on the clue our leprechaun left us."

The lesson continues and, once the sentences on the board are completed, each child is given a mimeographed sheet on which is written three sentences. Each sentence has a word with a shamrock drawn over all but the initial consonant. Students are told that the leprechaun left them each a surprise (Leprechaun picture to color and a puzzle are at the bottom of each sheet). Students are then asked to read each sentence, saying "blank" when they come to the shamrock and trying to figure out what will go in that blank that makes sense and begins with the clue left by the leprechaun. When they think they know what goes in each blank, they can come up and whisper the responses to the teacher and then telling no one else what their guess was, they can color the leprechaun and complete the puzzle he left for them.

As the students whisper in Mr. Jones' ear, he makes notes about two abilities, the ability to use context to come up with a response that makes sense in the sentence and the ability to use initial consonant letter/sound associations to figure out unknown words. As the morning goes on and Mr. Jones works with other groups, he continues to structure lessons and tasks which allow him to diagnose by observing which students can do what.

Because these observations occur as a natural part of the lesson, children are able to demonstrate their true ability unconfounded by the anxiety, panic, and inability to understand directions that often result from the knowledge that one is taking a test. Because the teacher has structured the observations so that decisions are based on the correct or incorrect responses of the children, the teacher views these responses in an objective, unbiased way. Because these observations are always conducted in the context of "real" reading, the teacher can observe not only whether or not students have learned certain associations, but also whether or not they can apply what they have learned as they read. Intuitive teachers achieve validity by objectively measuring what they choose to measure in a natural context which simulates as closely as possible the tasks children are actually required to perform as they read.

A Theory of Reading as a Guide to Diagnosis by Observation

At this point, you are probably asking yourself a very important question: How do intuitive teachers know what to measure and when to measure it? How do they decide which children need to be evaluated? The ability to know what they need to diagnose for students at differing stages of reading ability is what, in my belief, separates and distinguishes the intuitive teacher from the nonintuitive teacher. Even though few intuitive teachers will admit it, and many are not even aware of it, intuitive teachers have a theory of reading.

It is with fear and trepidation that I even mention the word, *theory,* much less assert that it lies at the heart of intuitive teaching. In teacher training and inservice, theory has become almost a dirty word. "Teachers need practical suggestions, teaching strategies they can use tomorrow," we are constantly told. Theory is seen as extraneous to successful teaching and learning.

The backlash against theory is an understandable and probably a justified phenomenon. In too many cases, teachers have been taught theory that had little or no applicability in classrooms. Even when the theory had applications to real teaching, the teaching of this theory was, like much teaching of reading, not taken to the application level. Professors *assumed* that teachers would be able to evolve strategies and implement classroom practices consistent with the theory they were taught. In many cases, this proved to be an erroneous assumption. The saying, however, that "there is nothing as practical as a good theory" is true if teachers have been taught how to apply the theory or if teachers have evolved a theory based on their careful, thoughtful, evaluation of the success and failure of various teaching practices with children at different stages of reading development.

Now, many of you may question the statement that intuitive teachers have a theory of reading. You may want to test my assertion by running out and stopping teachers on the way to the lunchroom and asking them to state in 100 words or less their theory of reading. The response you will get from these teachers will probably convince you that they not only don't have a theory of reading but are hostile to the whole idea of theory and to you! If, however, you really want to know if a particular teacher has a theory of reading, engage that teacher in a dialogue in which you ask questions such as: "What do you do when a child is reading and substitutes a word that doesn't change the meaning of what is being read?" or "Do children have to know letter names before they can begin learning to read some words?" or "Should a child who is in the fourth grade but is reading at the 2^2 level be allowed to point to the words while reading?" "What about finger-pointing for a child reading in the preprimers?" Intuitive teachers have answers to these questions. The answers may vary from teacher to teacher just as the theory held by teachers may vary. However, intuitive teachers can answer questions relating to how reading is learned, which abilities are prerequisite to others, and which reading strategies are appropriate at various levels of development. This practical theory held by intuitive teachers is not a set of abstract constructs but rather a set of beliefs which guide the intuitive teacher to ask the right questions at the right time.

Test makers also have a theory of reading. This theory is evidenced by the type of tasks included on the test. It is on this basis that intuitive teachers and test makers/promoters often part company. In buying a test, one doesn't just buy the how of measurement, one buys the what. A test does more than provide a way of measuring. A test, by its very being, determines what you will measure, whom you will evaluate, and when. If the theory of the test maker and the theory of the teacher are incompatible, the teacher is locked into not only testing but also teaching in a way which is "counterintuitive."

A Balanced Program of Diagnosis

You may have inferred as you read this article that I am unalterably opposed to any use of standardized or criterion referenced tests. Not so! Standardized tests serve the important function of giving us some information about the overall effectiveness of our reading program. I am not opposed to the use of standardized tests when the results of these tests are used as they were intended to be used—to make judgments about how *groups* of individuals are progressing toward meeting the various curriculum goals. I am opposed to the misuse of standardized test scores to make decisions about how *individual* children are progressing. Many test makers and test manuals will clearly state the the standard error of measurement inherent in the test renders the test results invalid as they relate to the progress of an individual.

I am also not opposed to the wise use of criterion and teacher-made tests when these tests are *selected* by the teacher who will use them. When a teacher selects a test which will give information about how various children are progressing toward achieving certain goals, the test selected is generally compatible with the theory of reading held by the teacher. Information gained from the administration of teacher-selected tests is apt to help that teacher make instruction decisions and support that teacher's intuitive judgments.

What I am opposed to is the systemwide, countrywide, or statewide imposition of a test package on all teachers. While the purchase and implementation of these neat, packaged, efficient systems hold tremendous appeal for parents, supervisors, administrators, school board members, and legislators, a growing number of "master teachers" stand firmly convinced that these systems are hindering rather than promoting good instruction. These systems often represent a short cut to the goal of improved reading instruction; the path of these systems may be shorter, but it may also be more hazardous; many could be lost to cliff and gulley.

Universally good diagnosis will become a reality when we have universally good instruction. Such instruction can become a reality only if we have universally good teachers. This article has attempted to describe what it is that intuitive teachers do. Through preservice and inservice training, our teachers can learn effective instructional techniques and can come to develop a theory of reading. They can be taught to make valid and reliable observations and to select tests consistent with their beliefs. The training of intuitive teachers will not be a quick, neat, manageable process, but the product will be as effective and as lasting as the process was long and painstaking. While the path may be longer, the coming home will be surer.

Reference

Nunnally, Jim C. *Psychometric theory.* New York: McGraw-Hill, 1967, 172-175.

The Quality of Reading Miscues

W. *Dorsey Hammond*
Oakland University

A central question in diagnosis of any reading performance is simply: How well does the student read? The question is commonly answered by the comprehension section of an informal reading inventory (IRI) which typically reports the results in terms of reading grade level. The means by which diagnosticians have arrived at a level of comprehension traditionally has been the answering of questions after oral or silent reading. A retelling procedure sometimes has been seen as an alternative to the use of questions and is currently being used and advocated by some diagnosticians.

There are two other informal approaches commonly used to diagnose reading performance: A word recognition in isolation test, and word recognition in context test. The word recognition in isolation score is obtained by having the subject read lists of words of increasing levels of difficulty. An alternate procedure used with word lists is to present each word in a "flash" and "untimed" mode. This method assumes that a correct response on a "flash" presentation is representative of a child's sight vocabulary, whereas the "untimed" presentation is representative of the reader's use of phonics. Despite the lack of empirical evidence to support the diagnostic utility of this procedure, it is nevertheless advocated by many reading diagnosticians.

The word recognition in context score seems to deserve more attention since it reflects the reader's performance with materials that are far less contrived and artificial than are lists of isolated words. The word recognition in context score is obtained by noting errors such as substitutions, omissions, and mispronunciations as the student reads orally. The results are usually reported as a percentage score that is obtained by dividing the number of words into the number of recorded errors. For example, if the passage is two hundred (200) words in length and the reader makes twenty (20) errors, the score would be ninety percent. There are, however, problems with the scoring of measures of word recognition in context. Diagnosticians have had difficulty deciding what constitutes an error—such as whether self-corrections, regressions, and meaningful versus non-meaningful substitutions are errors. As early as 1946, Betts pointed to the problem of determining just what constitutes a reading error. Harris and Sipay (1975) used a checklist to include detail and to weigh oral reading errors. Johns (1978) suggests counting all errors or miscues* and then subtracting dialect miscues, corrected miscues, and all miscues that do not change meaning for a net score of significant miscues.

Procedures such as those suggested by Harris or Johns which are designed to deal with the qualitative aspects of oral reading may be valuable, but they also seem somewhat over-simplified. The determination of whether or not an oral reading error affects meaning is not a one-dimensional consideration. For example, does the error change the meaning of the sentence? Is an error meaningful within the context of the story, but not meaningful within a given sentence? In short, the evaluation of oral reading is a fairly complex activity that must focus on the nature of the errors made and particularly upon the extent to which these errors distort the meaning of a passage.

In recent years, Kenneth Goodman and his colleagues have built a model of how reading takes place; and they proposed a comprehensive diagnostic approach for looking at oral reading miscues based upon that model. Publication of the Reading Miscue Inventory (RMI) by Y. Goodman and Burke (1972) is the result of the work they have done in the area of analyzing oral reading miscues.

* For the moment, the terms miscue and errors will be used interchangeably to refer to any instance where what is read is different from the text of what is being read. A rationale for why the term miscue is preferred will be developed in the next few pages.

The RMI is designed to serve as a diagnostic instrument for classroom teachers and clinicians; it is based on a model of reading which maintains that there are three cue systems used in reading: semantics or meaning clues, syntax or grammatical clues, and graphophonics or sound and visual clues. All three cue systems are used simultaneously by a mature reader and all three cue systems interact with one another. Another important part of the Goodman model stresses that meaning is both the *goal* of reading and a *means* by which one reads and recognizes words.

Goodman's Model of Reading, with which the RMI is consistent, is based on the study of hundreds of students reading orally from text. This intensive study of oral reading led to several conclusions:

1. Errors or miscues are not random, but follow a pattern.
2. Some errors or miscues appear to be more serious than others; in other words, some lead to a loss of meaning, others do not.
3. Errors or miscues are not the result of careless reading nor, in many instances, the result of poor reading since good readers also depart from text.
4. The same words can be cued correctly in one setting or context and miscued in another.

These findings led to the use of the term *miscue,* which seemed a descriptively better term than the commonly used term *error.* The research (Goodman, 1970; Goodman & Goodman, 1978) validated what many reading diagnosticians already intuitively knew— that errors or miscues don't just happen and that some miscues don't interfere with comprehension, and actually may enhance understanding, while other miscues reflect poor comprehension. Nevertheless, the term miscue seemed a more appropriate term since it sounds less judgmental.

The findings that miscues are seldom the result of careless reading and that words may be recognized in one setting and not in another suggest that the commonly held notion that a word is either known or unknown is not supportable. The findings further suggest that the process by which a reader identifies words cannot be fully explained by traditionally defined word recognition skills. In many, or most, cases what a reader produces orally is a result of the use of meaning, the anticipation of meaning, or of syntactical clues.

It is the balanced use of the three cue systems (meaning, syntax, and graphophonics) that identifies the effective reader. For example, too much reliance on word recognition or on contextual clues can be detrimental to the reading process. The following sentence illustrates the complex interactive nature of the three cues:

Soon his three sisters and two brothers would come home.

David, a fourteen-year-old, read the sentence as:

"Sun, his third sister and two brothers would come home soon."

Traditionally, one would count four errors in this sentence; however, much more is to be gained from a qualitative interpretation of David's miscues. In effect, he seems to have changed the word *soon* into the subject of the sentence and then he seems to have done what a good reader attempts to do: he changed *three* to *third* and deleted the *s* on *sisters*, which makes sense both semantically and syntactically. Merely scoring errors in this instance rather than noting a meaningful construction would penalize this reader for the use of a reasonable strategy.

The insertion of *soon* at the end of the sentence is more difficult to explain. My own interpretation is that it represents a simple insertion motivated by a desire for closure. It seems unlikely that he suddenly remembered that he had mispronounced *soon* and merely placed it at the end of the sentence. Nor does it seem likely that he suddenly swept his eyes back to the beginning of the sentence and "corrected" his first miscue. If this were the case, he would have most likely reread or paraphrased the entire sentence, which he did not.

Let's examine another example from David's oral reading. He had great difficulty with the following sentence:

And I, me, myself—I need a place of my own.

David struggled with the beginning four words of the sentence, yet most assuredly these are words he can recognize in isolation. Here he encountered difficulty because these words seldom appear in this particular syntactic configuration.

A miscue inventory, as exemplified by the Goodman and Burke RMI, allows for a qualitative interpretation to help ex-

Hammond

plain such reading behaviors. The RMI by Goodman and Burke (1972) asks nine questions about each miscue. They are:

1. Is it a dialect variation?
2. Is it an intonation miscue?
3. The extent of graphic similarity?
4. The extent of sound similarity?
5. The grammatical function of the miscue?
6. Is the miscue corrected?
7. The grammatical acceptability of the miscue (in context of prior and subsequent connected discourse)?
8. The semantic acceptability of the miscue (in context of prior and subsequent text)?
9. The extent of meaning loss?

Questions three and four deal with the relationships between letters and sounds, questions five and seven with grammar or syntax, eight and nine with meaning. Question six is particularly important because it asks if correction of the miscue was attempted. The reason readers correct a miscue is almost invariably because it either "doesn't sound right" or "doesn't make sense." Attention to grammar and meaning cause good readers to reprocess and, in effect, use good reading strategies to correct miscues. Miscue research strongly suggests that when good readers miscue, they err on the side of meaning; whereas, poor readers err on the side of phonics. One of the strengths of miscue analysis is in the breadth of the instrument; namely, that it is able to account for greater incidence of reader departure from text. The RMI allows for interpretations that are not possible with more traditional instruments.

An example of a fourth grade student illustrates another reason for analyzing miscues qualitatively. In a text of approximately 750 words this reader miscued more than 75 times. Yet, in the retelling of the text, about which he had limited prior knowledge, he was able to demonstrate a superb understanding of what he had read. His miscues were good miscues as opposed to bad miscues. One could argue, of course, that this reader is not a good oral reader, but one could not question the fact that he is a very good reader, because he comprehends what he reads.

After using miscue inventories for several years, I have reached the following conclusions:

1. The evaluation of word recognition in isolation is less

valuable than originally believed. The results of such evaluations are not particularly informative.

2. The word recognition in context score appears to have less value and validity than practice seems to suggest.
3. A systematic miscue inventory helps explain why students do what they do as they read.
4. Reading miscue analysis suggests that many children rely too heavily on phonic or graphophonic clues.
5. Miscue analysis provides insights into the reading process itself.
6. Miscue analysis has demonstrated the necessity of tape recording an oral reading performance in order to make reliable interpretations. It is impossible to code oral reading, for whatever purpose, simply by listening once as the child reads.

In practice, it is not necessary to administer miscue inventories to all students. However, intensive miscue training for classroom teachers and diagnosticians is strongly recommended since such training will significantly strengthen the ability of the teacher to draw diagnostic conclusions from observation during instruction.

In the history of diagnosis of reading performance, there have been significant advances made both in procedures and instruments. This writer regards the Reading Miscue Inventory as the most significant diagnostic instrument since the popularization of informal reading procedures over thirty-five years ago. Because of its theoretical base, its focus on the *process* of reading, its breadth in terms of accommodating all three cueing systems, and its focus on qualitative performance, the RMI procedure allows a much more adequate response to the question, "How well does a student read?"

References

Betts, E. *Foundations of reading instruction.* New York: American Book, 1946.

Goodman, K. Behind the eye: What happens? In K. Goodman, and Olive Niles, *Reading process and programs.* Urbana, Illinois: National Council of Teachers of English, 1970, 3-38.

Goodman, K., & Goodman, Yetta. *Reading of American children whose language is a stable rural dialect of English or a language other than English.* Washington, D.C.: Final Report, NIE C-00-3-0087, Department of HEW, 1978.

Goodman, Yetta, & Burke, Carolyn. *The reading miscue inventory.* New York: Macmillan, 1972.

Harris, A. J., & Sipay, E. *How to increase reading ability.* New York: David McKay, 1975.

Johns, J. *Basic reading inventory.* Dubuque, Iowa: Kendall/Hunt, 1978.

New Informal Approaches to Evaluating Word Recognition and Comprehension

Morton Botel
University of Pennsylvania

There are some who behave as though reading is a product—the sum of the separate skills measured by tests. In contrast, there are those who think of reading as a process—an aspect of the learner's continuous search for meaning. The second of these positions most closely represents the view of learning to read that will be taken in this paper. I believe that we enhance the search for meaning most productively through what might be called *holistic* reading-learning experiences, that is activities which treat reading as part of a meaningful language experience. Examples of productive holistic experiences include regular daily periods of listening to literature, self-selected reading, oral composing, and self-selected writing.

Likewise, it seems reasonable to think that we encourage and increase the search for meaning by helping the learner to get to *know* the workings of language through the processes of going from the whole of language to the parts and back to the whole again. Throughout these activities the emphasis is consistently on the learner's construction of meanings. This process of going from the whole to parts and then back to the whole again will be referred to as a *holistic/analytic/synthetic* process. Examples of productive learning experiences in this mode include closure or cloze type exercises, sentence making. (How many different sentences can be made by arranging and rearranging a selected group of words from a story?), word making (How many different words can be made by arranging and rearranging a selected group of letters or letter patterns from a story?), and learning to study informational material using a unified study approach, like SQ4R. It might be helpful to also illustrate activities that are not holistic in nature, but instead are illustrative of how reading skills are fractional. Learning an isolated group of sight words, learning how to "sound out" individual letters, studying "the" meanings of a list of words, and doing practice exercises on a so-called subskill of comprehension such as reading for details in a test-type format are all illustrations of nonholistic activities.

As students are engaged in holistic and holistic/analytic/synthetic language experiences, teachers can observe reading behavior, both word recognition and comprehension. This kind of observation is often called diagnostic teaching. As students engage in holistic experiences, such as the reading and oral rereading of passages of material or the oral reading of original student writing, word recognition and comprehension abilities can be demonstrated and observed in situations that are far less artificial and contrived than is frequently the case in evaluating reading skills. As Goodman (1979) has emphasized, and as Hammond points out in an earlier chapter of this volume, an observational focus on the reader as a searcher for meaning gives us a way of looking at errors or miscues in a way that allows the quality of the deviation to be taken into consideration. Thus errors which do not interfere with meaning, such as corrected errors, dialect variations, meaningful substitutions, and insignificant omissions can be discounted as compared with refusals and misreadings that do interfere with meaning. Observations of reading by teachers in classrooms over time clearly portray the learner in the most valid, reliable, and useful way.

There is some disagreement as to the minimal unit that can legitimately serve as the means of evaluating reading. In the following statement, Goodman and Page present their concerns with respect to evaluation using sentences and words rather than larger units of meaningful language.

The isolated word list test strategy described here is common in school systems. It is probably worse than no test strategy at all because the information it yields is confusing and misleading ... Reading is treated as though the performance of identifying isolated words by saying their sounds is the same as the reading process itself (Page, 1979, p. 75).

Reading tests frequently establish minimal reading situations which greatly impair the operation of one or more of the language systems. One common procedure is to introduce a sentence or short paragraph with one underlined word in it followed by several items, one of which is supposed to be a synonym for the underlined word (Goodman, 1979, p. 16).

I respectfully both agree and disagree with these statements. I agree that the fragmented view of reading mentioned earlier places too much emphasis on isolated elements and so-called subskills unsupported by science. I disagree with the statements because most linguists, cognitive psychologists, and psycholinguists have concluded that being conscious of how language operates is important in learning to read. This language awareness is developed when the learner works on aspects of decoding at the syllable, word, and sentence level. For example, in one analysis of the research in beginning reading instruction, Gibson and Levin (1975, pp. 323-324) concluded that the beginning reader already has skills of gaining information using syntactic and semantic clues, but needs to develop conscious awareness of the relationship between letters and sounds because "there is nothing in language behavior or other content previously acquired by the child that will transfer to this aspect of the reading task." Their specific reference to the sentence and word as an appropriate basis for instruction is: "The child should encounter sentences from the very beginning of training, because the sentence is the minimal unit that 1) insures comprehension and 2) provides all three types of information [semantic, syntactic and graphophonic]. A differentiation model will be followed, that is, the complete sentence will be introduced first and then will be broken down into its component parts."

In another comprehensive review of research sponsored by the National Institute of Education to determine what we know today about reading instruction, Weaver (1978) also concluded that direct instruction in decoding should be a primary focus of early reading instruction.

There are seven research findings that seem especially supportive of the use of instructional strategies based on a holistic/analytic/synthetic mode of language experience. These findings also have implications for the evaluation of reading skills. These findings are:

1. It is conceptually easier to learn to recognize words as representing meaning directly rather than as representing consonant and vowel sounds (Goodman, 1979; Rozin, Poritsky, & Sotsky, 1971).

2. It is easier to recognize words in context than in isolation (Goodman, 1979).

3. At the same time the search for meaning is encouraged, attention of the learner should gradually be focused on the relationship between letters and sounds, sometimes called the graphophonic principle. In learning this principle, the syllable is a more concrete perceptual unit and, therefore, a more learnable unit than the phoneme (Gleitman & Rozin, 1977; Liberman et al., 1977; Rozin & Gleitman, 1977).

4. The young reader should acquire "a set for diversity," i.e., an understanding that a letter may stand for more than one sound (Gibson & Levin, 1975, p. 324).

5. The general ability to recognize words in isolation at the primary levels is highly correlated with the ability to recognize these words in context. Furthermore, the ability to read spelling pattern syllables and nonsense words is highly correlated with general reading comprehension. Such a correlation does not suggest that we ought to teach words in isolation or to practice decoding by using nonsense words (Calfee, Chapman, & Venezky, 1972; Shankweiler & Liberman, 1972).

6. Vocabulary knowledge is highly correlated with general reading comprehension (Anderson & Freebody, 1979).

7. General reading comprehension cannot be reliably subdivided into subskills, not even into the skill of deriving explicit meaning and the skill of deriving implicit meaning (Mason, Osborn, & Rosenshine, 1977).

These seven research findings suggest principles for designing objective measures for determining: 1) the reading instructional levels of students and 2) mastery of the global patterns of English spellings represented by the ability to recognize high frequency syllable/spelling pattern words in lists or in sentences.

An Earlier Approach to Informal Evaluation

A short history of my search for general measures for an instructional level for reading and for a measure of mastery of English spelling patterns follows:

In the early 1950s I developed three subtests that became the Botel Reading Inventory (1978). With only one reading/ English consultant for Bucks County Schools in Pennsylvania (some 45,000 students) there was a pressing need to have some realistic ways for helping classroom teachers determine the instructional levels of their students. Since almost all of our teachers used basal readers and since it was found that over 25 percent of our elementary school students were placed in basal readers at their frustration level, the placement of students at their correct instructional level became a very important program objective.

After trying various approaches, a combination of a word recognition test (as an estimate of oral reading fluency) and a word opposites test (as an estimate of silent reading comprehension) was found to be a valid, reliable, and useful battery for the correct placement of students in basal readers.

The Word Recognition Test included preprimer through fourth level word lists sampled from the Botel 1180 Common Words (Botel, 1976), derived from a frequency study of the common words in five major basal readers. The ability to read aloud correctly at least 70 percent of the words in a list was regarded as mastery at the indicated level. This score corresponded to 95 percent oral fluency *in context* (obviously context helps). Uncorrected mispronunciations and refusals were counted as errors.

The Word Opposites Test included first reader through senior high school words sampled from the Botel 1180 Common Words and the Lorge Thorndike Word Book of 30,000 Words. The ability to read silently and correctly identify at least 70 percent of the word opposites was regarded as indicating mastery at the indicated level.

As a measure of mastery of the major patterns of decoding, The Phonics Mastery Test of the Botel Reading Inventory sampled four levels of decoding: Level A—Beginning Consonants, Blends, and Rhyming Words; Level B—Vowel Sound/Spelling Relationships; Level C—Multisyllabic Words; and Level D—Multisyllabic Nonsense Words. The first three levels corresponded roughly with the graphophonic content of typical basal readers at the time in grades one, two, three. The format for determining knowledge of phonics in Levels A and B was the ability to write the first letter or vowel sound heard in a word. I later came to believe that the ability to read syllables was the more valid means for determining knowledge of the alphabetic system and the new Botel Reading Inventory (1978) represents that view.

In addition, during the same time period, I developed a criterion system called the Cooperative Reading Checkout for advancing students from one level of their basal reader to the next. Essentially this involved a collaborative decision between the teacher and the principal whenever the teacher believed the students had mastered a given level of the basal. Mastery was defined as reading in the last unit of the basal reader with at least 95 percent fluency in the oral reading of stories with at least 75 percent comprehension in silent reading. Oral reading errors were defined as mispronunciations or refusals. Repetitions, insertions, and substitutions were not regarded as errors for the purposes of meeting the criterion if the meaning of the passage was not essentially changed. Comprehension was judged by average performance on workbook pages dealing with comprehension done independently by the student at that level.

Given one or both of these procedures, teachers were encouraged to observe student performance in daily tasks and modify instruction and placement accordingly.

These procedures still seem reasonably valid and most parsimonious with respect to the management problems of classroom teachers and in the larger context of a comprehensive reading/language arts instructional framework.

In more recent years as I continue my search for efficient, useful, and time-economizing ways of testing students, I developed and am researching two additional procedures for obtaining criterion referenced measures of student reading competence. These are: 1) the Botel Milestone Tests (BMT), and 2) a procedure for developing a maze test for placement/mastery in any basal reader program.

Principles for Constructing the Botel Milestone Tests (BMT)

The seven research findings cited earlier in this paper formed the basis for the derivation of four general principles on which the BMT is built. These four principles are:

1. Tests of reading should be constructed so as to use the sentence as the primary unit of testing since the sentence includes semantic, syntactic, and graphophonic clues and since the sentence is a convenient unit.
2. General reading comprehension skill can be estimated through the use of a vocabulary-in-context approach. Such an approach is recommended because no scientific distinctions can be made in determining the subskills of comprehension and since a vocabulary measure is more predictive of general comprehension than any other measure of general comprehension. To put it another way, a vocabulary-in-context measure is not just a vocabulary test, it is the ideal surrogate test for general comprehension.
3. Two groups of tests should be constructed—one to determine the student's ability to recognize the most common words in sentences and to decode the most common syllable/spelling patterns, and one to determine the student's ability to comprehend increasingly difficult material.
4. To achieve validity and reliability the words for the sentences should be randomly chosen or some other means should be used to obtain a *representative* sample of words. Valid studies of frequency of word use and semantic knowledge of students at various grade levels should be used. The preprimer word recognition test should be developed from the Botel 1180 Common Words (1976), the decoding tests from the *American Heritage Word Frequency Book* (Carroll, Davies, &

Richmond, 1971), and the advanced comprehension tests from Dale and O'Rourke's *Living Word Vocabulary* (1976).

A brief description follows each of the subtests (and two examples of each subtest) of the Botel Milestone Test. Each subtest is read silently. The mastery criterion for each subtest is 90 to 100 percent. A score of 70 to 80 percent on a subtest suggests that subtest level is the student's instructional level. Sixty percent or lower is regarded as indicating frustration at that level.

FOUNDATION SUBTESTS:
DECODING/COMPREHENSION (1-3)

Functional Subtest A: Decode and comprehend sentences composed only of words commonly found in basal readers at the preprimer level (e.g. *little, jump, play*).
1. Is mother in the   up   house   me?
2. I have a big blue   ball   red   for.

Functional Subtest B: Decode and comprehend sentences in which most words have the regularly spelled CVC (short vowel) pattern (C = consonant, V = vowel), such as *web, mad, log*.
1. Mom and Dad dug in the   mud   ill   met.
2. Pam sells her pots and her   nods   pans   sits.

Functional Subtext C: Decode and comprehend sentences in which most words have the regularly spelled CVCe (long vowel) pattern such as *cage, pipe, tide*.
1. Pete is hiding the tire in the   wise   cave   cane.
2. Jane rode the bike to the   lake   mate   wake.

Functional Subtest D: Decode and comprehend sentences in which most words have the semi-regularly CVVC patterns, including the vowel sounds other than long or short such as *cow, toy, noon;* the *r* controlled vowel such as *tar, dirt, form;* and the alternate (other than those in Subtest B) spellings of the long vowel sounds such as *beef, tea, sail.*
1. Ray paid for the meat with the   mood   coins   calm.
2. At noon he will feed hay to the   joy   sigh   cows.

Functional Subtest E: Decode and comprehend sentences in which most words have the regularly spelled CCVCC (short vowel) pattern and CCVCCe (long vowel) pattern (cc = consonant clusters, V = vowel) such as *twist, crash, shade, slope*.
1. At camp Jack slept in a   frog   tent   luck.
2. Gwen put the silk belt on the   grade   shine   dress.

Functional Subtest F: Decode and comprehend sentences in which most words have the semi-regularly CCVVCC and CCVVCCe patterns including the vowel sounds other than long or short such as *mount, shoot;* the *r* controlled vowel sound such as *storm, march;* and the alternate (other than those in Subtest E) spellings of the long vowel sounds such as *brain, feast, flight.*

1. Mark spread the creamy cheese on the
   <u>blow</u>   <u>bread</u>   <u>burst.</u>
2. Jean fainted when she saw the   <u>doubt</u>   <u>teach</u>   <u>ghost.</u>

ADVANCED SUBTESTS: LEVELS OF COMPREHENSION (4-12)

Functional Subtest G: Comprehend word meanings in sentence contexts at fourth and fifth grade levels.

1. The teacher *admires* good students.
   <u>thinks well of</u>   <u>settles down</u>   <u>puts blame on</u>
2. His gambling left him *broke.*
   <u>like a boy</u>   <u>very smart</u>   <u>without any money</u>

Functional Subtests H, I, J, and K would successively evaluate the comprehension of word meanings in sentence contexts at grade levels: six and seven, eight and nine, ten and eleven, twelve and thirteen. The format of the test would be the same as that for Level G; increasingly more challenging vocabulary items would be used.

Procedures for Construction of a Clozure Type (Maze) Test for Instructional Placement

I have outlined the second new approach I am proposing for determining a student's instructional level in any basal reader. An example of such a test then follows.

1. Choose a story or a coherent part of a story (more than one, if you want alternate tests) in the last unit of each booklevel, beginning at the primer level (there are too few words in the preprimer). The story segment should be approximately 100-200 words long.
2. Delete selectively 10 to 15 percent of the words in the story. Choose words for deletion that were introduced in the basal at that booklevel (words introduced at a booklevel are usually listed in the appendix of the book).
3. Type this story, leaving a long blank line for each word deleted. This should be long enough for three words.
4. On each blank line, type the word deleted and two foil words. Take the foil words from the list of words introduced in that booklevel or the previous level.

5. Have other persons read your test to check for ambiguity, awkward language, or items showing a bias of any kind.
6. Have the test typed or printed in readable type.
7. Before giving the test, instruct the students on how to take such tests; use sample paragraphs at a lower level of difficulty. Instruct the students to: 1) read the paragraphs or story segment all the way through, 2) sentence-by-sentence, choose the correct word from those on each line, and 3) mark the correct word.
8. Consider a score of 80 percent to 90 percent on a test to be strong evidence that the student has mastered that level, i.e. can read books at the next higher level at least. Consider the first level at which the student falls below 80 percent to 90 percent to be his instructional level.
9. Administer this test near the beginning of the year to place students in basal readers and administer it again to confirm mastery of each level when teachers believe students have successfully completed each level.
10. When the teacher's observational judgment of a particular student's achievement is not confirmed by the test, the situation should be studied further. One option is to give the student the test individually as an oral reading test. Or the teacher might confer with a facilitating teacher or an administrator who has also observed the child.

2^2 Level

---

name   date

BABY HERCULES AND THE GIANT SNAKES*
Little Hercules' mother tucked him and his twin brother into their <u>crabs</u> <u>cribs</u> <u>drawer</u>. "Good night, babies," she said as she put out the light. Then, just as she closed the bedroom door, two giant snakes, pythons, came <u>though</u> <u>throw</u> <u>through</u> the open window.

---

*From *Explorations,* in D.C. Heath, *Reading,* by Morton Botel, John Dawkins, and Alvin Granowsky, 1973.

In the moonlight sunlight bedtime the babies saw the snakes coming toward them. Soon the huddle huge huggable pythons would wrap themselves afraid arrow around the baby boys.

"Mommy! Mommy!" Hercules' brother cried. He tried tied told to get out of his crib. Their mother, hearing the screams, ran quietly quickly queerly toward their room.

"Mommy! Mommy!" Hercules' brother cried again. But the baby Hercules wasn't a bit afraid. He stood up and wasted waited worked quietly. And when the pythons came near, he grabbed them by their necks near next and held them.

By the time their mother opened the door, she saw the snakes thrashing their giant baskets babies bodies back and forth. Baby Hercules was holding one in each hand.

Conclusion

The most valid, reliable, and useful approach for the informal appraisal of word recognition and reading comprehension is observation of the reader reading in naturalistic settings over time. Documentation of oral and silent reading in self-selected materials, reading one's own compositions, reading plays, and rereading textual material portrays the many faces of word recognition and comprehension.

In addition teachers and schools typically want an objective criterion-referenced measure of the student's competence in word recognition and comprehension. Given the unreliability of tests of subskills below the level of the syllable in word recognition and below the level of general comprehension, diagnostic tests at these sublevels fail to meet the requirements of science. Instead, milestones tests of general competence in word recognition and comprehension can be developed to provide helpful information for placement and for planning instruction. Several procedures I have developed for this purpose represent some of the options available.

References

Allen, P. D., & Watson, D. J. (Eds.). Findings of research in miscue analysis: Classroom implications. Urbana, Illinois: Eric Clearinghouse on Reading and Communication Skills and National Council of Teachers of English, October 1976.

Allington, R. L., & McGill-Franzen, A. Word identification errors in isolation and in context: Apples vs. oranges. *Reading Teacher*, 1980, *33*, 795-800.

Anderson R. C., & Freebody, P. *Vocabulary knowledge*. Technical Report No. 136. Champaign, Illinois: University of Illinois at Urbana-Champaign, 1979.

Botel, M. *How to teach reading*. Chicago: Follett, 1976.

Botel, M. *Botel reading inventory, administration manual*. Chicago: Follett, 1978.

Botel, M. *Botel milestone tests*. Philadelphia: Botel-Sheppard, 3458 W. Penn Street, Philadelphia, Pennsylvania 19129, 1980.

Brooks, L. Visual pattern in fluent word identification. In A. S. Reber, and D. L. Scarborough (Eds.), *Toward a psychology of reading*. Hillsdale, New Jersey: Erlbaum, 1977.

Calfee, R., Chapman, R., & Venezky, R. How a child needs to think to learn to read. In Lee W. Gregg (Ed.), *Cognition in learning and memory*. New York: John Wiley, 1972.

Carroll, J. B., Davies, P., & Richman, B. *Word frequency book*. New York: American Heritage, 1971.

Dale, E., & O'Rourke, J. *The living word vocabulary*. Chicago: Field Enterprises Educational, 1976.

Gibson, E. J., & Levin, H. *The psychology of reading*. Cambridge, Massachusetts: MIT Press, 1975.

Gleitman, L. R., & Rozin, P. The structure and acquisition of reading I: Relations between orthographies and the structure of language. In A. S. Reber, and D. L. Scarborough (Eds.), *Toward a psychology of reading*. Hillsdale, New Jersey: Erlbaum, 1977.

Goodman, K. S. Emergence of new methodology for reading instruction. In K. S. Goodman, (Ed.), *Miscue analysis: Applications to reading instruction*. Urbana, Illinois: Eric Clearinghouse on Reading and Communication Skills and National Council of Teachers of English, 1979.

Liberman, I. Y., Shankweiler, D., Liberman, A. M., Fowler, C., & Fischer, F. W. Phonetic segmentation and recoding in the beginning reader. In A. S. Reber, and D. L. Scarborough (Eds.), *Toward a psychology of reading*. Hillsdale, New Jersey: Erlbaum, 1977.

Mason, J. M., Osborn, J. H., & Rosenshine, B. V. *A consideration of skill hierarchy approaches to the teaching of reading*. Technical Report No. 42. Champaign, Illinois: University of Illinois at Urbana-Champaign, 1977.

Page, W. D. Clinical uses of miscue research. In K. S. Goodman (Ed.), *Miscue analysis: Applications to reading instruction*. Urbana, Illinois: Eric Clearinghouse on Reading and Communications Skills and National Council of Teachers of English, 1979.

Rozin, P., & Gleitman, L. R. The structure and acquisition of reading II: The reading process and the acquisition of the alphabetic principle. In A. S. Reber, and D. L. Scarborough (Eds.), *Toward a psychology of reading*. Hillsdale, New Jersey: Erlbaum, 1977.

Rozin, P., Poritsky, S., & Sotsky, R. American children with reading problems can easily learn to read English represented by Chinese characters. *Science*, 1971, *171*, 1264-1267.

Shankweiler, D., & Liberman, A.M. Misreading: A search for causes. In J. F. Kavanagh and I. G. Mattingly (Eds.), *Language by ear and by eye: The relationships between speech and reading*. Cambridge, Massachusetts: MIT Press, 1972.

Weaver, Phyllis (with Fredi Shonkoff). *Research within reach*. Newark, Delaware: International Reading Association, 1979.

The Cloze Procedure as an Informal Assessment Technique

John J. Pikulski
and
Aileen Webb Tobin
University of Delaware

Although the cloze procedure was originally introduced as a technique for assessing readability (Taylor, 1953), its uses as an evaluation tool for reading have expanded in many directions within the past two decades. The cloze procedure possesses the following characteristics which are frequently associated with informal evaluation procedures for reading: 1) it can be teacher-constructed rather than being in published form, 2) it can be constructed from materials that might be used for instructional purposes, 3) it uses preestablished standards to judge the adequacy of an individual's performance rather than comparing an individual's performance to some normative standards, and 4) it can yield information that can be helpful in making decisions about the levels at which a student might best profit from instruction.

For the reasons mentioned above, these authors feel that a strong case can be made for viewing the cloze procedure as an informal evaluation tool for reading. However, for those who narrowly equate informal evaluation (clearly not the position in this volume) with informal reading inventories, the cloze procedure will seem very different from informal methods. While IRIs are individually administered, cloze tests are typically group administered; while IRIs take samples of reading material from texts without altering the form of that material, cloze procedures require changing the text by omitting some of the words; while IRIs tend to rely heavily on oral reading to evaluate word identification or decoding skills, cloze evaluation materials tend to be silently read; while IRIs assess comprehension through asking questions that tend to rely on both understanding of the material and memory for the material, cloze procedure assesses the ability to use grammatical and meaning clues to fill in the missing parts of a message.

Thus, the position taken in this paper is that the cloze technique is one of the many informal approaches that can be taken to measure reading. The striking differences that exist between cloze and informal reading inventories make cloze an ideal compliment to a full informal inventory. Because IRIs are individually administered, and they comprehensively evaluate reading skills through a variety of approaches, they serve best as highly diagnostic instruments that yield information useful for making judgments about individual children. However, the very advantages of IRIs immediately present a disadvantage—they are very time-consuming to administer and require much diagnostic skill for adequate interpretation. In contrast, since cloze is a group procedure it can be administered very quickly and efficiently to large numbers of students. The results from a cloze test are also interpreted in a fairly straightforward fashion; however, like most group procedures, cloze sacrifices the ability to make detailed diagnostic observations and it lacks the precision of results that can be achieved through individually administered instruments. For these reasons it is best to think of the cloze procedure as a screening device that efficiently and quickly yields results that must be viewed as tentative.

In spite of a tremendous amount of research involving cloze as an evaluative procedure, as might be expected, there are still many unanswered questions about how effective the procedure is as a diagnostic tool and the form that cloze procedures should take. Some of the questions surrounding the effectiveness of cloze will be addressed in the later sections of this paper; the bulk of the paper will focus on the various practical approaches that have been suggested for the use of this technique.

Description of the Cloze Technique

The term cloze was introduced by Wilson Taylor in 1953. It is derived from the word closure, which is a concept borrowed from the gestalt school of psychology. This school of psychology developed in an attempt to explain the complex phenomena of perception. The psychological approaches developed to that date seemed at a loss to explain the difference between what actually was occurring (sensations) and what human beings tend to perceive. For example, what in reality is a series of individual pictures, rapidly shown and varying only slightly, is perceived as a picture with movement. A mosaic is really a large number of individual pieces of material, yet it is perceived as a picture. Through a study of complex perceptual phenomenum, the gestalt psychologists arrived at a series of perceptual "laws," one of which was the law of "closure" which stated that when a familiar object is presented with some detail lacking, there is a psychological tendency to see that object as a whole unless a deliberate attempt is made to find a missing part.

Taylor reasoned that the same psychological tendency would exist with respect to written materials—that if there were missing pieces, there would be a natural psychological tendency for people to fill in the gaps to try to achieve a complete whole. For example, given the sentence "I think I'll go for a walk in the _____," there are a number of words that immediately come to mind—yard, park, woods, water, night, sun. The familiarity of the language and context of the sentence create a tendency to want to close or complete the sentence.

In effect, cloze is a way of measuring how familiar the reader is with the language and content of the material to be read. From another point of view, it is a way of measuring the closeness of the language and background of the author and the reader; the closer the match between the two, the easier the reading material will be. For example, many of you reading this book would have little difficulty in filling in the missing word for the sentence: "The combinations ch, sh, and th, are all illustrations of _____." Because many of you bring a backgound in reading with you, you probably are able to identify the missing word as being *digraphs;* however, given the sentence, "Annealing with a _____ laser beam was introduced in 1974 by Russian scien-

Pikulski and Tobin

tists," many of you might have trouble filling in the missing word *pulsed* because you're not familiar with the technology of microelectric devices. In short then, cloze is a method whereby words are omitted from sentences and a reader is asked to fill in the missing words. The form that cloze takes will vary depending on the purposes for which it was constructed.

Uses for Cloze

Although there is some evidence to suggest that the cloze procedure might be used as an alternative to standardized tests of reading achievement (see Bickley, Ellington, & Bickley, 1970; Rankin, 1974), most reading specialists and consultants tend to concur that it can be more profitably adopted for the following purposes:

1. *To assess the readability of material.* While much of the material in this volume focuses on the evaluation of the skills a reader possesses, there is constant concern in the field of reading about evaluating the difficulty of reading materials as well. The most frequent approach taken to evaluating the difficulty in readability of materials is the use of readability formulae. However, most of the popular readability formulae appear to have serious limitations and most tend to rely solely on some measure of word difficulty (either number of syllables in the word or the fact that a word is not on a list of common words) and on sentence complexity which is usually measured through sentence length. Because of the restricted nature of these formulae, it is impossible for them to measure factors such as the use of an unusual meaning for a common word, highly symbolic language, awkward and confusing sentence structure, the rate at which new ideas are introduced or the use of illustrations to support the development of an idea. In effect, readability formulae tend to be rather static, over-simplified approaches to trying to measure the difficulty a piece of material will present for a reader. One other important consideration is that readability formulae fail to consider the background of experience that a reader possesses for reading a particular piece of material. As

noted earlier, most readers of this chapter will be far more successful reading materials related to the field of reading than in reading about microelectronic technology. Cloze has the distinct advantage as an approach to readability of allowing a direct assessment of the interaction of readers with reading materials. All of the factors which will make a piece of material easy or difficult will influence whether or not an individual or group of people will be able to fill in words that have been deleted from a selection. In his original work, Taylor (1953) found a high rate of agreement between readability formulae and cloze in ranking the difficulty of three passages which appeared to contain few of the factors beyond word length and sentence length that influence readability; however, when he compared the rankings of three passages which deliberately violated some of the assumptions underlying the use of common formulae, cloze proved a more adequate measure of readability.

The use of cloze as a measure of readibility will probably remain limited because it does not yield the traditional grade level scores that many teachers and reading specialists have come to expect. Through the use of cloze scores, passages or books can be ranked from easiest to most difficult but not categorized as fourth or sixth reader level. There is a roundabout way for assigning a grade score based on cloze, but this will be explained later in the chapter after the discussion of the construction, scoring, and interpretation of cloze tests.

2. *To place students in basal reader series and other types of graded, instructional materials.* When cloze is used for this purpose, it is probably most like an IRI in function. The test materials can be constructed by selecting one or more passages from each of the texts that are being considered for instructional use. By administering selections from several reader levels it becomes possible to *estimate* a student's independent and frustration levels. (Criterion scores for determining functional reading levels are presented and discussed later in this

chapter.) The differences between the use of cloze for *estimating* an instructional level compared to diagnostically *establishing* an instructional level from an IRI has already been mentioned.

There is, however, some research which allows for an estimate of the amount of agreement likely between establishing an instructional level from cloze as compared with an IRI. There is evidence (Cunningham & Cunningham, 1978; Jones & Pikulski, 1974) that the two will agree 70 to 80 percent of the time. Thus, cloze procedure seems a very reasonable screening device for instructional placement in reading.

3. *To evaluate the appropriateness of content area texts.* Given the practical utility of the cloze procedure as a technique for placing students in basal readers, it is perhaps not surprising that content area teachers are often encouraged to use this procedure to select texts that are written at an appropriate level of difficulty or to try to identify those students who may need special help or support in order to be able to profitably use a text. However, while it seems reasonable to assume that content area teachers should have no difficulty adapting cloze to screen their students for instructional placement, it is usually inappropriate to assume that it will enable them to place their individual students in texts written at their instructional levels. Even when teachers have the option of placing their students in more than one text, it is often necessary to choose a text that is poorly suited to the reading ability of a large number of students. This is partially due to the fact that students are usually assigned to content area classes without considering either the range of differences in their reading ability or the range of materials that are available to the teacher. But it is also a matter of practicality: texts differ in their content and organization, and teachers who are expected to teach a variety of classes simply lack the time to vary their instruction accordingly.

Thus, in many instances, cloze can be recommended only with the expectation that it will help content area teachers select texts appropriate for the majority of the students in their classes. However, it may also suggest the need for some small group work involving discussion of vocabulary and concepts central to the content to be read before this group of students is expected to complete reading assignments, especially when the assignments are to be completed independently.

A major advantage to the use of cloze in content areas lies in the fact that it is relatively simple to construct, administer, and score. Many content area teachers simply do not have the background to allow them to use more complex assessment procedures. There is also the obvious advantage of allowing for group administration of this procedure.

Types of Cloze Tests

Conventional, random deletion cloze tests. As suggested, the purpose of the evaluation often determines how a cloze test might be best constructed, administered, and scored. When the purpose of the evaluation is any of the three just discussed (to measure readability, place students in appropriate reading materials, or assess readers' abilities to cope with the demands of content area texts), teachers are usually advised to use a random deletion cloze. In this form of cloze test (probably the most commonly used form), every fifth word is deleted, regardless of the word. In some variations of this procedure, it is recommended that every seventh or tenth word be omitted. The random deletion form of cloze has been the subject of a great deal of research and is very easy to construct, administer, and score.

Construction of random deletion cloze tests. Recommended procedures for constructing a random deletion cloze test are as follows:

1. Select a passage of approximately 250-300 words. This passage should appear to be representative or typical of the content of the book. If the book becomes progressively more difficult, try to select a passage from the second quarter of the book.
2. Inspect the passage to insure that it is not heavily dependent on information presented earlier in the text.

If it contains a number of anaphoric words and phrases (e.g., it, this, these, points) which have referents found only in earlier sections of the text, another passage should be selected.

3. Keep intact the first and last sentences.
4. Randomly choose one of the first five words in the second sentence. Beginning with this word, omit every fifth word until 50 words have been deleted. A word is defined as any group of letters set off by spaces. Thus, a number such as 1980 should be deleted as if it were a single word. However, hyphenated words are generally considered two separate words, except in instances where the prefix cannot stand alone as in co-opt.
5. Replace the deleted words with blanks of uniform length, and number each of the blanks consecutively.
6. Prepare an answer sheet that the students can use to record their responses.

To illustrate the form that a random deletion cloze test takes, the next paragraph of this chapter is written in the form of cloze test. It is an abbreviated form in that it has 15 rather than the recommended 50 blanks. If you have never taken a cloze test, you might find it interesting to try to fill in the missing words. You would probably find it helpful to list the numbers 1 to 15 on a piece of paper and write next to each number the word you think should be inserted in the corresponding blank. The omitted words are listed at the end of the paragraph.

The decision to delete every fifth word is based on both practical and empirical considerations. In addition to the _1_ that it can be _2_ adopted to construct a _3_ number of test items _4_ a reasonably short passage, _5_ Taylor (1956) and MacGinitie _6_ have provided evidence to _7_ that an every-fifth-word _8_ pattern provides the maximum _9_ of context necessary to _10_ reliable responses. Leaving more _11_ four words between the _12_ blanks had no effect _13_ the restoration of missing _14_ and, thus, no apparent _15_ . The obvious disadvantage to using every sixth or seventh, etc., word is that students need to read longer passages in order to respond to 50 deletion items.

Omitted words are: 1. fact 2. easily 3. large 4. from 5. both 6. (1961) 7. suggest 8. deletion 9. amount 10. elicit 11. than 12. cloze 13. on 14. words 15. advantages

Using a 250-300 word passage is also a recommendation based on experimental evidence. Generally, a 250-300 word, 50-item cloze passage can be expected to yield a reliability coefficient in the neighborhood of .85 (Bormuth, 1975). Although this seems sufficient for most of a teacher's purposes, it must be emphasized that an individual's score on a test having a reliability coefficient of less than .90 cannot be interpreted with a great deal of confidence. At best, it represents only an estimate of the students' ability to deal with the demands of the material. However, it seems somewhat impractical to recommend that the teacher select a longer passage since it would be necessary to double the number of test items in order to raise the reliability to a minimum of .90 (Bormuth, 1975).

In addition, a cloze test based on a 250-300 word passage has several practical advantages. A passage of this length happens to fit comfortably on a single sheet of paper and, as a result, it is likely to encounter less student resistance than tests constructed from longer passages. Also, it is easy to calculate percentage scores on a 50-item test—simply multiply by 2.

Administration. If students have had no previous experience with cloze, it is advisable to do a practice exercise. This exercise should be constructed from materials that are fairly easy for the students to read and should consist of approximately 10 items. To conserve time and facilitate group discussion, the exercise may be written on the board or displayed with an overhead projector.

Instructions will differ depending on the age of the students and the type of cloze test that is to be administered. When a random deletion cloze is being used, the following directions or some variation might be used:

Some words have been left out of these sentences. Your job is to fill in as many of the missing words as possible. Some of the later sentences may give you clues about the earlier ones. The best thing to do is to read through all of the sentences first, and then go back to the beginning and try to fill in the blanks. Only one word goes in each blank.

After the students have had sufficient time to read the passage, individual students should be asked for possible answers. Any answers that are meaningful and syntactically correct should be accepted. This should help students recognize that there are, at times, several reasonable choices for filling in the blanks. If an answer does not seem reasonable (e.g., *it* instead of *they*, when a plural noun is the referent), the clues that might be used to help the students choose a more appropriate response should be discussed.

Once the introductory exercise has been completed, copies of the cloze test should be distributed to each of the students, along with the following advice:

> Although this exercise is similar to the one we have just completed, you will very probably find it more difficult. No one is expected to answer all of the items correctly. Try to choose the words you feel best complete the sentences, and remember to write only one word in each blank. You may skip hard blanks and come back to them when you have finished. If you are not sure how a word should be spelled, give it your best try. Wrong spelling will not count against you.

If numbers, contractions, or hyphenated words have been deleted from the passage, the students should also be given some representative examples of the types of answers that can be used to fill in the blanks. Although students should be encouraged to work as long as they please, the teacher may want to set a time limit when it appears that their efforts are no longer productive.

Scoring. One of the most seriously misunderstood aspects of using a random deletion cloze is that students should be given credit only for answers that are exact (verbatim) replacements of the missing words. Words with spelling errors may be considered correct as long as it is evident the student intended to write the word originally deleted. But no credit should be given for synonyms or other types of substitutions (*girls* for *girl, walk* for *walked*) even though they may seem somewhat acceptable.

The decision to use verbatim as opposed to synonym scoring is based on a considerable amount of experimental evidence as well as practical considerations. A number of researchers (Gallant, 1964: McKenna, 1976; Miller & Coleman, 1967; Ruddell, 1964; Taylor, 1953) have compared exact replacement scores with various types of synonym counts and have concluded that the latter are not worth the extra time and effort. Synonym counts tend to yield slightly higher correlations with other measures of reading comprehension (Gallant, 1964; McKenna, 1976), but they also tend to be less reliable since they are based on subjective judgments of what is and what is not an acceptable response. In addition, it appears that there is absolutely no advantage in giving credit for synonyms when the purpose of the evaluation is to obtain an estimate of students' abilities to meet the demands of material. Although synonym counts tend to yield higher scores than exact replacement counts, correlations between the scores derived from the two types of techniques usually exceed .95 (McKenna, 1976; Miller & Coleman, 1967). Consequently, it can be assumed that students will be ranked in almost exactly the same way, regardless of the manner in which their answers are scored. If synonyms are accepted, the teacher or specialist will be forced to require a much higher percentage score as a standard of acceptability, thus the student really achieves no advantages.

However, the primary reason for recommending that the teacher accept only exact replacements is really very simple: There are no available guidelines for determining the students' functional reading levels when more subjective scoring procedures of accepting synonyms are adopted. As might be assumed, the criterion scores derived are based on the assumption that the student has been given credit only for answers identical to the words appearing in the original passage. Somewhat higher standards would obviously need to be established if synonyms were considered acceptable responses.

Interpretation. Several different strategies have been adopted in attempting to derive criterion scores for judging student performance on random deletion cloze exercises. Bormuth (1967, 1968) used two types of measures—examiner-constructed, multiple-choice comprehension tests and an expanded version of the Gray Oral Reading Tests—to determine comparable independent and instructional level scores on random deletion exercises. The results suggested that cloze scores of 57 and 44 percent accuracy correspond to comprehension scores of 90 and 75 percent—the comprehension standards that traditionally have been adopted for evaluating independent and instructional reading levels. Rankin and Culhane (1969) replicated Bormuth's work in a study comparing cloze with other multiple-choice tests and reported very similar results.

However, Bormuth (1968, 1969, 1971) and others have also provided some evidence to suggest that these criteria may not be the most appropriate standards to adopt when other variables are taken into consideration. For example, when Bormuth (1968) used oral reading accuracy as the criterion for determining comparable levels of cloze performance, he found that somewhat lower cloze scores might be used as the standards for judging independent and instructional reading levels. The results of this analysis indicated that cloze scores of 54 and 34 percent were comparable to the conventional standards for independent (98 percent) and instructional level (95 percent) performance on measures of word recognition. Similarly, studies comparing student performance on IRIs and cloze exercises have generally suggested somewhat less stringent criteria for converting cloze scores into equivalent functional reading levels. Both Ransom (1968) and Jones and Pikulski (1974) concluded that the following criteria approximate the results obtained on IRIs: independent, above 45 percent; instructional, 30-45 percent; and frustration, less than 30 percent.

To confuse the issue even more, we feel we should point out that Bormuth (1971) has also conducted research which suggests that higher standards need to be adopted if the amount of information to be gained as well as the novelty of the material and the students' willingness to study and rate of reading are to be considered in selecting appropriate reading materials. In order to maximize the value of each of these variables, Bormuth suggested that cloze scores should fall within the range of 49 to 59 percent when the material is being considered for instructional purposes.

Obviously, much more research needs to be conducted to resolve some of the discrepancies in the criterion scores that have been suggested. However, for the teacher's purposes, it appears that the following criteria might be adopted as reasonable starting points in evaluating student performance on random deletion cloze tests:

Independent level: Students who obtain cloze scores of at least 50 percent should be able to read the material with relative ease. No teacher guidance should be necessary. Consequently, this material should be appropriate for homework assignments and other types of independent projects.

Instructional level: Students scoring between 30 and 50 percent should be able to use the material for instructional purposes. However, some guidance will be necessary to help them master the demands of the material.

Frustration level: Students having scores of less than 30 percent will usually find the material much too challenging. Since there is almost no potential for success, the material should be definitely avoided.

While these criteria are suggested as beginning points, teachers and reading specialists may need to adjust them based on the experience they have with cloze. Again, there is some evidence to suggest that more stringent criteria than those listed above should be used.

At this point it seems appropriate to point out that when using cloze as a measure of readability one could roughly attach a grade level designation to a text if a cloze test were administered to a group of individuals of known reading ability. For example, if it were known that a group of students were reading at about a fourth grade level and if on the average they scored about 45 percent on a cloze test from a particular book, one could say that the book was about at a fourth grade level.

Additional Uses for Cloze

A modification of the conventional, random deletion cloze is necessary when cloze is used for purposes other than the three previously discussed. For example, cloze can be used to evaluate student mastery of content area instruction or for diagnosing the student's ability to use various types of contextual clues. When the cloze procedure is used for these purposes, it is usually recommended that the teacher prepare an exercise in which the words are deleted on a rational rather than a mechanical basis. Examples of rational deletion cloze exercises will follow.

In addition to the fact that only key words are deleted, rational deletion cloze tests differ in that synonyms are now accepted as correct. If the exercise is to be used to diagnose the student's strengths and/or weaknesses, or to assess how much he/she has learned, the teacher would certainly want to accept synonyms for scoring a rational deletion cloze. Verbatim scoring is necessary only when one wishes to establish functional reading levels, to assess readability, or to evaluate content materials.

Pikulski and Tobin

Some of the uses and forms that rational deletion cloze tests can take follow:

Using cloze to gain a clearer perception of the student's ability to use contextual clues as an aid to word recognition. Although much more research needs to be conducted to determine its diagnostic capabilities, it is generally assumed that cloze can be used to gain insight about the student's ability to use various types of syntactic and semantic clues. When it is adopted as a diagnostic tool, it is recommended that the teacher construct separate exercises for each of the skills that are of interest such as recognition of pronoun antecedents, subject-verb agreement, and semantic relationships. Selected portions of exercises that might be used to assess some of these skills are presented below:

Pronoun antecedents: Bill and Henry loved to play tricks on ____ sister. Once Bill mailed Judy a large, blank canvas and asked ____ to enter it in the local art show. Judy was surprised when ____ saw what ____ planned to enter, and. . . .

Semantic relationships: The koala bear is one of the most helpless of all wild ____. Whenever there is any sign of danger, koalas become very ____. Usually, they climb to the ____ of a tree and stay there until everything seems ____ again.

The diagnostic utility of these and similar exercises depends, of course, on the care with which the exercises are constructed and the student's responses are analyzed. As these illustrations suggest, the words to be deleted need to be carefully selected in light of the specific purpose of the exercise. For example, if the teacher is interested in evaluating the student's ability to use pronoun antecedents as a clue to word recognition, only those pronouns that seem to have definite antecedents should be deleted. The deletion of pronouns that do not have any identifiable referents will not only make the exercise frustrating for the student to complete but will also increase the probability of making an inaccurate diagnosis.

Similarly, it seems critical that teachers select passages which will enable them to construct exercises having relatively large numbers (25-50) of deletions. As in all forms of evaluation, the confidence one can place in the results depends on the length of the measure: the greater the number of deletions, the easier it is to assume that the exercise will provide an adequate sample of the student's skill in using a particular type of contextual clue.

In addition, it is suggested that teachers select passages written at the student's independent or, at most, instructional level. This should reduce the possibility of concluding that the student needs to become more aware of particular types of contextual information when the difficulty lies only in the student's ability to recognize the words appearing in the exercise.

Finally, we feel we should again emphasize that it would be inappropriate to evaluate students' needs for additional instruction simply by comparing their responses to the exact words deleted from the material. While reproduction of the exact word is required when cloze is used to screen students for instructional placement, it clearly does give students credit for responses that reflect their ability to use various types of contextual clues. For example, the first blank in the passage about koala bears might be appropriately clozed by a number of words—creatures (the word that was actually deleted), animals, or bears.

Unfortunately, there are no established guidelines for determining which responses should and should not be considered acceptable. Nor are there any guidelines to indicate how many of the students' responses need to be considered acceptable in order to assume they have mastered the skill being evaluated. While these are issues that are not easily addressed, they are hardly peculiar to the cloze procedure. Teachers who rely on other types of informal techniques (classroom observations, teacher-constructed mastery tests) to diagnose their students' strengths and weaknesses are constantly confronted with the problem of establishing appropriate criteria for instructional mastery.

Using cloze to assess student mastery of the content of a particular instructional unit. Although there is virtually no empirical evidence to suggest that cloze can be used to evaluate the effectiveness of content area instruction, it seems reasonable to assume that it can be used for this purpose if the following precautions are adopted. First, the teacher should either select or prepare a passage which summarizes the concepts under consideration. Second, only key or important words should be deleted. Third, the students should be given credit for synonyms and other types of substitutions which are indicative of their

Pikulski and Tobin

understanding of the concepts that are being evaluated. To the extent that the students' errors are not simply a reflection of their ability to recognize the words appearing in the exercise, the results should help the teacher assess the overall quality of the instruction that has been provided as well as the need for review and reinforcement.

Additional Variations of the Cloze Procedure

Maze technique. One of the more popular variations of the basic cloze procedure was first suggested by Gallant (1964, 1965). She reasoned that it would be preferable to use a multiple-choice format with young children since they might have difficulty recording their answers on conventional cloze exercises. Guthrie, Siefert, Burnham, & Kaplan (1974) also suggested the use of a multiple-choice cloze procedure to monitor growth in reading and to guide the selection of reading materials. This procedure requires the reader to choose the words that constitute the most sensible path through a verbal "maze"—hence, the term, maze technique. The following illustrates the form a maze test might take:

	evaluation		for
"Cloze is one	label	that has been recommended	to
	procedure		him

	prefer
a wide variety of	purposes."
	errors

The maze technique has both advantages and disadvantages. Its primary advantage is that children find it less difficult and hence less objectionable than conventional cloze. Likewise, it requires less time to administer. Its disadvantages are that it is much more time-consuming to construct and has been subjected to far less research.

Guthrie and his colleagues suggest that the teacher adopt the following guidelines for constructing, administering, and scoring a maze test:

1. Select a representative passage approximately 120 words in length.
2. Replace every fifth word with three alternatives. These alternatives should include: a) the word originally de-

leted; b) a distractor which is the same part of speech as the deleted word; and, c) a distractor that is syntactically different from the omitted word. (No guidelines have been established to indicate how close in meaning the distractors should be to the correct choice. For practical purposes we suggest that, where possible, the teacher choose the distractors by scanning a previous page of the material being used to construct the maze, and selecting words that fit the criteria for being a distractor.)

3. Vary the alternatives so the correct answers do not appear in the same position throughout the exercise.
4. Distribute copies of the exercise to students and have them circle the correct choices.
5. Give students credit only for the selection of exact replacements.

The criteria to be used in interpreting the results of a maze exercise seem somewhat more tentative than the standards that have been suggested for random-deletion cloze. Guthrie et al. suggested that "if a child is performing at about 90 percent accuracy for three or four administrations of the maze, more difficult material should be introduced. Optimal teaching levels are about 60 to 70 percent accuracy (p. 167)." Thus, an independent level on the maze would be 90 percent and above, an instructional level 60 to 69 percent, and a frustration level below 60. However, Pikulski and Pikulski (1977) have provided some evidence to suggest that these criteria may need to be raised when they are used with regular classroom students. In a study comparing the maze scores of 61 fifth graders with teacher judgments of students' functional reading levels, they found that the maze technique overestimated students' reading ability more than 45 percent of the time. These results differed significantly from those obtained in a preliminary study (Pikulski, 1975) conducted with reading disabled students attending the University of Delaware Laboratory School. When working with reading disabled students, the standards recommended by Guthrie et al. appeared to be appropriate.

Similarly, the reliability and validity of the maze technique have not been well-established. To our knowledge, only three studies have addressed these issues. Guthrie (1973) used the data collected on a group of 36 children, ranging in age from seven to ten years, and found that none of the internal consistency reliability coefficients for each of seven passages fell below .90. He also reported a correlation of .85 between maze and the Gates-MacGinitie Vocabulary Test and a correlation of .82 between maze and the Gates-MacGinitie Comprehension Test. Similarly, Bradley, Ackerson, and Ames (1978) reported moderately high correlations among alternate forms of the maze, constructed by different teachers and administered to second graders. However, Bradley and Meredith (1978) also concluded that it may be inappropriate to use maze for assessment at the intermediate and junior high levels when it is administered in its typical format. In a study of fourth, sixth, and eighth grade students (N = 335), they found that the cloze procedure tended to place subjects either at the instructional or frustration level, while parallel forms of the maze produced a ceiling effect, placing students predominantly at the independent level. To increase maze score variability and, thus, its reliability and overall ability to detect differences in reading achievement, the investigators suggested that the following modifications be considered: " a) discarding the option type (i.e., distractor) utilizing a syntactically incorrect word; b) devising new option types (e.g., semantically correct within sentence but semantically incorrect within passage); c) increasing the number of options per item" (p. 188).

Post-oral reading cloze. Another variation of the basic cloze procedure is the post-oral reading cloze test developed by Page (1977). This type of cloze test is constructed in exactly the same manner as the conventional, random-deletion cloze. The only difference is that students are asked to read the intact passage orally, before they are administered the cloze material. Page suggested that this procedure provides a valuable link between the evaluation of oral reading and reading comprehension. Based on Page's research, one should expect a post-oral reading cloze to yield scores that are 10-20 points higher than conventional cloze scores.

Limited cloze. In an attempt to provide teachers with a more appealing alternative to conventional cloze, Cunningham and Cunningham (1978) have developed another type of multiple-choice procedure. This procedure is called limited cloze because it differs from the conventional, random deletion procedure only in one respect: the deleted words are randomly ordered and listed above the passage, providing the student with a limited number of choices to insert in the blanks. Words deleted more than once are listed at the top of the test as many times as necessary, and students are informed that each of the words in the list can be used only once to fill in the blanks. As in the conventional procedure, only exact restorations of the original words are scored as correct.

The Cunninghams have suggested that limited cloze has several advantages. In addition to the fact that it is easy to construct and administer, it also has the advantage of reducing some of the resistance often encountered when teachers are asked to use verbatim scoring procedures. Also, limited cloze avoids the problem of developing appropriate distractors—an issue that is often raised when the maze technique is adopted. And finally, it appears that limited cloze is as valid and reliable as conventional, random-deletion cloze. In two separate studies, the Cunninghams found that limited cloze tests yielded substantially higher internal-consistency coefficients than conventional cloze passages: .85 versus .64 in one study, and .90 versus .70 in the other. They also found that limited cloze scores correlated more highly with the comprehension subtest of the Iowa Tests of Basic Skills than did those obtained with conventional cloze although the difference in the validity coefficients was not significant.

The major limitation of the limited cloze is that it yields scores that are not easily converted into functional reading levels. In their preliminary work with the limited cloze, the Cunninghams found that it yielded an instructional range of 60 to 81 percent in one study and a range of 73 to 93 percent in another. Whether a reliable instructional range can be established remains an issue for subsequent research.

Conclusions

The forms cloze tests can take and the uses for which they can be employed vary considerably. Hopefully, this chapter has pointed to ways in which this procedure can be flexibly used as an informal evaluation tool. While cloze has been subjected to substantial research during the past two decades, teachers and reading specialists must recognize that it is not a totally reliable or valid way to measure reading skills but, certainly, this is a caveat that could be applied to virtually every other approach to evaluating reading. Overall, cloze appears to have many advantages, so that it seems reasonable to conclude that it can be used profitably as one approach to informally evaluating reading skills.

References

Bickley, A. C., Ellington, Billie J., & Bickley, Rachel T. The cloze procedure: A conspectus. *Journal of Reading Behavior*, 1970, *2*, 232-249.

Bormuth, John R. Cloze test readability: Criterion reference scores. *Journal of Educational Measurement*, 1968, *10*, 291-299.

Bormuth, John R. Comparable cloze and multiple-choice comprehension test scores. *Journal of Reading*, 1967, *10*, 291-299.

Bormuth, John R. Development of standards of readability: Toward a rational criterion of passage performance. USOE Technical Report No. 9-0237. U.S. Office of Education, 1971. ED 054 233.

Bormuth, John R. Empirical determination of the instructional reading level. In J. Allen Figurel (Ed.), *Reading and realism*. Newark, Delaware: International Reading Association, 1969, 716-721.

Bormuth, John R. The cloze procedure: Literacy in the classroom. In William D. Page (Ed.), *Help for the reading teacher: New directions in research*. Urbana, Illinois: Eric Clearinghouse on Reading and Communication Skills, 1975.

Bradley, John, Ackerson, Gary, & Ames, Wilbur. The reliability of the maze procedure for classroom assessment. *Journal of Reading Behavior*, 1978, *10*, 291-296.

Bradley, John, & Meredith, Keith. The reliability of the maze procedure for intermediate and junior high school students. In P. David Pearson and Jane Hansen (Eds.), *Reading: Disciplined inquiry in process and practice*, Twenty-Seventh Yearbook of the National Reading Conference. Clemson, South Carolina: National Reading Conference, 1978.

Cunningham, James W., & Cunningham, Patricia M. Validating a limited-cloze procedure. *Journal of Reading Behavior*, 1978, *10*, 211-213.

Gallant, Ruth. An investigation of the use of cloze tests as a measure of readability of materials for the primary grades. Unpublished doctoral dissertation, Indiana University, 1964.

Gallant, Ruth. Use of cloze tests as a measure of readability in the primary grades. In J. Allen Figurel (Ed.), *Reading and inquiry*, Newark, Delaware: International Reading Association, 1965.

Guthrie, John, Seifert, Mary, Burnham, Nancy, & Caplan, Ronald. The maze technique to assess, monitor reading comprehension. *Reading Teacher*, 1974, *28*, 161-168.

Jones, Margaret B., & Pikulski, Edna C. Cloze for the classroom. *Journal of Reading*, 1974, *17*, 432-438.

MacGinitie, Walter H. Contextual constraint in English prose paragraphs. *Journal of Psychology*, 1961, *51*, 121-130.

McKenna, Michael C. Synonymic versus verbatim scoring of the cloze procedure. *Journal of Reading*, 1976, *20*, 141-143.

Miller, G. R., & Coleman, E. B. A set of 36 prose passages calibrated for complexity. *Journal of Verbal Learning and Verbal Behavior,* 1967, *6,* 851-854.
Page, William D. Comprehension and cloze performances. *Reading World,* 1977, *17,* 1-12.
Pikulski, John J., & Pikulski, Edna C. Cloze, maze, and teacher judgment. *Reading Teacher,* 1977, *30,* 766-770.
Pikulski, John J. The maze technique for estimating the instructional level of disabled readers. Unpublished manuscript, University of Delaware, 1975.
Rankin, Earl F. The cloze procedure revisited. In Phil L. Nacke (Ed.), *Interaction: Research and practice in college-adult reading,* Twenty-Third Yearbook of the National Reading Conference. Clemson, South Carolina: National Reading Conference, 1974.
Rankin, Earl F., & Culhane, Joseph. Comparable cloze and multiple-choice comprehension scores. *Journal of Reading,* 1969, *13,* 193-198.
Ransom, Peggy E. Determining reading levels of elementary school children by cloze testing. In J. Allen Figurel (Ed.), *Forging ahead in reading.* Newark, Delaware: International Reading Association, 1968.
Ruddell, Robert B. A study of the cloze comprehension technique in relation to structurally controlled reading material. In J. Allen Figurel (Ed.), *Improvement of reading through classroom practice.* Newark, Delaware: International Reading Association, 1964.
Taylor, Wilson L. Cloze procedure: A new tool for measuring readability. *Journalism Quarterly,* 1953, *30,* 415-433.
Taylor, Wilson S. Recent developments in the use of the cloze procedure. *Journalism Quarterly,* 1956, *33,* 42-48, 99.

Informal Diagnosis of Content Area Reading Skills

T. Stevenson Hansell
Wright State University

Educational diagnosis, the act of learning about skills that a student possesses prior to instruction, is a step which logically follows a clear description of the goals a teacher holds for a class of students. Goal setting, making decisions about concepts and procedures that students should master, must serve as the basis for sampling and evaluating student behavior. It is on the basis of established goals, and through diagnosis, that a teacher makes such important decisions as what to include; how to relate new concepts to past experiences; the rate and sequence of instruction; choosing instructional procedures that lead to effective and efficient learning; and, finally, selecting materials that will contribute to the achievement of goals. The establishment of goals must be the step *before* diagnosis since using testing instruments before goals clarification will fragment the instructional effort. Once goals have been established, however, a teacher can intelligently select and design informal procedures which will measure student performance in relation to selected goals. Thus, diagnosis is an intermediate step between the description of long range goals and the development of short-term objectives.

Instructional goals are established on the basis of a teacher's knowledge, philosophy, attitudes, and abilities, as well as teaching environment. Most likely, the goals adopted by the content teacher will vary little regardless of student skills and abilities. Therefore, informal diagnostic measures should serve as valuable tools in allowing teachers to understand the skill levels that students bring with them to content materials.

A distinction is frequently drawn between diagnosis and evaluation. Diagnosis often refers to some type of formative or preinstructional information collection, whereas, evaluation more commonly describes postinstructional information collection. However, the distinction is necessarily a somewhat artificial one because of the need for ongoing diagnosis to make needed adjustments in short-term instructional objectives. Postinstructional evaluation should not only evaluate the student's previous learning, but it should also suggest needs for future instruction; in other words, frequently evaluation and diagnosis will take place simultaneously using the same information. The distinction is not better clarified if one examines the types of tasks or materials used in diagnosis or evaluation. In fact, the proposals made in this chapter suggest the use of content-relevant tasks and texts as the basis of both diagnosis and evaluation. The true difference separating diagnosis and evaluation is the purpose for which they are done. Diagnosis should help with future instructional decision making, and evaluation should measure the accomplishment of previous goals and objectives. Because of the similarities in methodology, the terms diagnosis and evaluation will be used interchangeably in this chapter. It is left to the reader to decide the purposes toward which these techniques will be used.

The purpose of this paper is to show that reading goals are often content specific; the accomplishment of some reading goals are integral to the overall goals of the content.

Learning to Read and Reading to Learn

When content teachers have a list of behaviors a student cannot do (identify sequence, form hypotheses, and identify root words), a frequent reaction is, "Send these kids back to me when they can read." This reaction is understandable when viewed from the perspective of a teacher whose long range goals treat the deficient skills as only peripherally a part of his or her responsibilities.

To understand the role of reading instruction in the content area classroom it is important to distinguish between the goals of the reading teacher and those of the content area teacher. The differences between teacher goals for content reading and for basal reader reading are partly differences of emphasis. When students read a basal reader, the teacher more frequently focuses on such concepts as word recognition and comprehension. That is, a reading teacher focuses on teaching each student *how* to understand words and passages. In content area instruction when students read a textbook, teachers frequently focus exclusively on the product of reading or *what* to understand. Thus, when assigning content reading, teachers sometimes disregard the *how to*.

Because of the different goals of authors who write basal readers and authors who write texts, there are clear differences in the vocabulary the authors use. Basal readers are generally written to contain only those words used frequently in written and spoken language. Most publishers have stepped away from strict vocabulary controls, but most basal series still rely on a core of words which are presented, repeated, and reviewed for several years. On the other hand, authors of content and reference books select words to represent the ideas they want to communicate. When the idea or concept is new to an individual student, the words will be new also. Thus, the vocabulary of the content text is both more varied and more technical than that of the basal reader.

While reading teachers should provide instruction in *how to* identify important vocabulary and *how to* make sense of text, it is appropriate that the content teacher keep the major focus on the ideas of the content. A content teacher may encourage the application of context, structural analysis, phonics and dictionary skills, but the use should be restricted to the needed vocabulary terms. Similarly, the content teacher may work with students to outline a passage, but the focus will remain on the ideas represented within the passage with outlining seen as a means to this end.

A second difference is that informational materials are written in a different style than stories. Such stylistic differences (i.e., less narrative, more exposition in content materials) assume different reader purposes and they entail differences in the tasks of understanding. For example, the narrative style of a story is inappropriate for mathematical thinking. Similarly, the listing style of a recipe is inappropriate for learning to think about history as a reflection of human behavior. A goal of content teachers, related to this difference of style, is that students learn how to think about a specific topic. To accomplish this goal some reading instruction must proceed from materials which legitimately require students to think about the content of interest.

The expectations a student develops from extensive exposure to story or narrative style writing lead a reader to select details about characters, events, and ideas in relation to an abstract idea of plot (Stein and Nezworski, 1978). The expectations of a math, science, or unified arts teacher, however, are that frequently each step must be mastered as a firm foundation for successive concept construction. For a student to be successful, he/she must learn a new mental set or scheme (Fredericksen, 1975) of expectations for different writing styles along with a plan for recognizing writing style and the topic before he/she reads. In short, each student must learn to exchange the treat-events-lightly-build-meaning-from-sequences style of reading, which is appropriate for basal stories, for the stop-reread-learn-and-then-proceed style which is necessary to understand new ideas presented in content reading.

Given the differences of vocabulary and style, and their impacts on the purposes and processes of reading, teachers find that students require guidance in the comprehension of content reading. This guidance or instruction is appropriate *within content classes* where the teacher goals include, first, an understanding of the content and, second, an increase in each student's ability to read *in the field of study*. Diagnosis based on a teacher's content area goals can clarify what instruction, including reading instruction, will be helpful for each student. Thus, diagnosis is a means to the end of better pupil understanding.

Approaches to Measuring Comprehension

Once a teacher has established clear goals for concepts and attitudes he/she wishes to address, it is appropriate to examine ways to measure what a student already knows and how well that student can understand a printed description of new ideas.

However, the problem arises in selecting appropriate informal measures because of a lack of agreement about what comprehension is and how it can be measured. Simons (1972) has discussed seven different approaches to measuring comprehension. Three of the seven (the measurement, factor analysis, and correlation approaches) will not be discussed here because they deal with formal or standardized tests. The remaining approaches include: a) the readability approach, b) the skills perspective, c) the introspective report, and d) the models approach.

Readability approach. The concept of readability is attractive for its simplicity. Readability ratings are an attempt to somehow measure the difficulty of a book. Since every teacher has watched a youngster flounder through some book, it makes sense to try to find a book that each student can read and understand without so much effort that the student quits before completing the task. However, the practice of readability measurement does not work as teachers would hope (Hansell, 1974, 1976a, 1976b).

Formulae such as those by Dale and Chall (1948), Fry (1968), and McGlaughlin (1969) focus on things which can be easily counted in a book—letters, words, syllables, sentence length, affixes, and so on. These countable items reflect less than five percent of what people have said make a book easy to read (Gray & Leary, 1935). As a result, it would not be surprising to find that a book with a readability rating of 7.3 is easier to read than one rated 6.8 for some students. Similarly, obviously all seventh grade students will not be able to read and understand a book with a readability rating of 6.8. As teachers know, students differ on any dimension we choose to measure. There is no guarantee that we can match readability levels of books and standardized reading test scores accurately.

Readability does not provide information about how youngsters will read a text or their familiarity with the topic treated in the text (Kintsch & Vipond, 1978). Comprehension, however, is the result of a meaningful interaction between the student and the text. In this process both student and text are important. Readability formulas may serve to sensitize teachers to examine books more closely, but if they lead them to ignore the students' approaches to this particular text their use might be destructive. A better way to determine the readability of a text might be to use some of the informal procedures described later in this paper.

Skills perspective. In contrast to readability formulae which focus on the text, the focus of the skills approach is on each student. The skills of content reading have been defined by analyzing classroom tasks and, thus, are practical. The skills approach to informal evaluation of content reading ability is most common by far; virtually every text on elementary, content, or secondary reading includes a list of so-called skills.

These lists range from what Herber and Riley (1979) call the "simplest form" of 1) vocabulary, 2) comprehension, and 3) reasoning, to a composite list which includes the following topics:

identify main idea of paragraph
identify main idea of selection
summarize
outline
put ideas in sequence
details of paragraph or passage/grasp directly stated details
locate information
make inferences
follow directions
draw conclusions
appreciate character
understand setting
recognize author's purpose
identify attitudes that the author is trying to convey
identify words the author chooses to achieve purpose
define key words
define words in context
syllabify
accent
identify meaning of affixes
identify meaning of roots
use synonyms, antonyms
choose best definition from dictionary
sense variation among words
identify part of speech
recognize sentence structure
recognize paragraph structure
see relations among ideas in passage
   time and place—events
   main idea—details
   compare—contrast
   hierarchy
   cause—effect
apply theoretical information
apply ideas

determine relevance of ideas
determine accuracy of information
think through the passage/anticipating outcomes
organize ideas
using parts of a book
  contents
  index
  glossary
  introductory paragraphs
  biographical data
note taking
use of card catalogue
use of dictionary
knowledge of indexes and abstracts

    The skills perspective generates such informal evaluation instruments as observational checklists, placement test (coordinated with materials such as workbooks, kits, basal readers, taped programs) and a wide variety of teacher-designed tests. Guidelines provided by Burmeister, 1978; Shepherd, 1978; Strang, 1964; and Thelen, 1976 reflect this type of approach. With variations they tend to suggest that teachers administer a group inventory including 20 to 35 questions about: 1) the book in general (size, shape, color, length, organization into chapters and units); 2) parts of the book; 3) vocabulary (which may be from the dictionary, knowledge of synonyms to define terms, and use of context); 4) word recognition (limited to syllabication, accent, and meaning of roots and affixes); and, 5) comprehension and rate of reading. Burmeister suggests five questions about each of three comprehension categories: details, main ideas, and questions which require students to interpret and use information from the text. Shepherd would add questions about sequence of events and drawing conclusions to which Strang would add organization of details and following directions.

    Simons' critique (1971) of the skills approach to comprehension seems to apply to the skills approach to evaluation:

    1. There is confusion about what can be called reading comprehension. Most observers would probably agree that the ability to relate ideas in a passage is vital to reading comprehension and, therefore, should be evaluated. But what about skills such as notetaking or selecting the best definition from a dictionary? These skills, although useful, would probably generate a

greater amount of disagreement among professionals. Obviously, those skills which are thought to be a part of reading, and of the content area subject, need to be taught, and should be evaluated. evaluated.

2. Another criticism leveled by Simons is that skills lists often contain global or poorly defined terms. This points out that one person's "recognizing a sequence of events" is another person's "recall of details." Various authorities might agree that a particular type of question should be included in an assessment; but because these skills lists are the subjective products of arm-chair logic, there are going to be gaps, overlaps, and disagreements over terminology.

3. Simons' final criticism is that there is no distinction between the product of comprehension (outlining) and the processes by which the product is achieved (identifying main ideas).

4. The skills approach suffers from other limitations as well. Another problem with the skills approach is that such tests may fragment the process of learning unnecessarily. If, for example, a student can outline a passage from a text, he/she can obviously identify main ideas, locate details, draw conclusions, and perceive the organization of ideas within the passage. Conversely, if a student cannot outline a text, there is little evidence available that working on one or more of the skills mentioned above will transfer directly to the task of outlining. The assessment of content area reading should probably begin with more global tasks (completing a recipe or outlining a passage) and then become more specific in intent if students are unable to successfully complete the task.

5. A final limitation of the skills approach is its focus on the student as opposed to the text or task. As has been noted, comprehension is best described as the product of a meaningful interaction of a student *and* text. This approach suggests to some that skills lists refer to genuine internal abilities of the individual which have little to do with a specific task or content area. Such perceptions often lead to assessments that are irrelevant to the task of interest. For example, the teacher who relies on the results of a general vocabulary knowledge test to specify which students are apt to have difficulty with the technical vocabulary in the biology text might be badly misled. Certainly, both the general vocabulary and the specific technical vocabulary fall within the area

of vocabulary knowledge, but this skill would not be expected to generalize. The best content area assessments require students to carry out tasks similar in complexity to what will typically be expected of them, using similar materials, and their performance of these tasks is then used to suggest what instructional steps are necessary to accomplish the instructional goals.

Introspective report. In contrast to the product oriented skills perspective, the introspective approach focuses on what the student has done to reach the goal, on what a student feels is easy or difficult about reading, and on each student's study habits. Strang suggests that after students have read an assignment in class they should be asked questions such as:

> What did you do to get the main idea?
> What did you do to remember the details?
> What did you do when you met a word you didn't know?

While introspective questions may help a teacher gain insight about each student's reading, the act of introspection is not without problems. A basic question raised by Simons concerns the relationship between the actual process of identifying main ideas and the verbal description. The same process may be described in several ways, but a change in description does not change the actual process. Students may also describe different mental operations by using the same words.

Introspective accounts are also retrospective. That is, students are asked to describe the reading process *after* they have read. Perhaps, introspective statements (of how main ideas were identified, for example) are influenced by the fact that the passage has been completed.

The introspective perspective is different from the skills perspective in that it focuses on the *process* of understanding as opposed to the *products* or answers. At the same time, the introspective measures may deal with many of the same aspects of content reading (main ideas, details, and vocabulary). As with the skills approach, the teacher gains the greatest information when requiring students to complete tasks with the specific content materials of interest.

The models approach. The models perspective of comprehension differs from the other approaches in its attempt to interrelate what may be described as separate skills and to explain the interrelationships of the comprehension process and product. Models of comprehension frequently take the form of flow charts or diagrams (Singer & Ruddell, 1976). One of the most explicit models of understanding discourse is a computer program designed by Winogard (1974) which can follow directions, and answer questions. Emphasis on models of comprehension is an attempt to come a step closer to the goal of developing one or more theories of how people understand information. The models approach suggests viewing student behavior in a variety of reading-thinking situations on the basis of the relationships and concepts that are part of a specific model of reading. This approach treats reading comprehension as a global, integrated act, and not just as a set of unique and diverse skills. The difficulty with a models approach to diagnosis is that teachers must understand a theoretical model before they can use it to test and guide instruction. In addition there is no theory of reading which can be considered complete at this time.

Diagnostic Instruments

For classroom use, the best method is the combination of approaches which is easiest and provides the most usable information. In classroom or clinical use, many distinctions between approaches disappear. Nonetheless, the following section is designed to present sample diagnostic instruments based on stated goals and to point out how each approach may add to a teacher's repertoire. The first section will deal with sampling vocabulary knowledge from the skills, introspective, and models viewpoints. The second section will show how these approaches might assess reading comprehension.

Sample vocabulary instruments

Situation: Ninth grade general English class
Goal: Increase students' ability to communicate and understand by
    increasing general vocabulary knowledge
Diagnostic choices:
    I. Skills approach
        A. For each of the words below, underline the root word and
           list three to five words which have the same root.
           1. vision
           2. bicycle
           3. perimeter

B. Define each underlined word in the sentences below according to the way it is used in the sentence.
1. As I walked home from the football game, I had a *vision* of what life could be like in 2050.
2. The *perimeter* of the army camp was well guarded.
C. Select the best dictionary definition for the underlined word in each sentence.
1. According to the paper, we can now *bicycle* in the park.
   a. n. a vehicle usually designed for one person consisting of a frame, two wheels, a seat, handlebars for steering, and two pedals on a motor by which it is driven.
   b. intr. v. to ride or travel on a bicycle.
   c. adj. having two cycles.

II. Introspection
A. What does it mean to you when I say, "The *perimeter* of the wheel is 63 centimeters."
B. Rate each of the following words on a scale of 1 to 4.
   Let 1. mean I've never heard of it.
        2. mean I've heard of it but can't define it.
        3. mean I can define it if I hear it in a sentence.
        4. mean I know it. I can define it, and I can use it.
                                              (Dale, 1978)

III. Models approach
A. List as many words as you can think of that are associated in any way with the following words.
   Example: *milk*, cookies, chocolate, white, cow, dairy, farmer, baby, cheese, sour, ice cream, butter . . . .
B. List all the ways you can find in which the objects represented by the following words are alike.
   bicycle, car, log, trailer, sewing machine, eyeglasses, dime . . . .
C. Play Dictionary Poker or Glossary Guesswork by trying to write a definition on a 3 x 5 card for one of the following words which you do NOT know. Your definition will be mixed with other students' definitions. The real definition will also be added. Each student will then have a chance to vote on which definition he/she thinks is "real." One point is awarded for each student who guesses your definition (i.e. each person you fool). Two points are awarded to each person who correctly votes for the "real" definition.

These first examples were based on diagnosing vocabulary knowledge as separate from reading comprehension. Though the examples relate to general vocabulary, the formats can be directly adapted to any content area. Instead of "bicycle," the same tasks could be carried out with *protractor, proton,* or *proletariate.*

One factor should be apparent about informal vocabulary measures of the introspective and models types: there are no single "correct" answers. The personal meaning, the rating, the association task, finding similarities, and Dictionary Poker all require a student to actively search and organize thoughts in relation to a vocabulary term. If these activities are inconsistent with teacher goals, then the instruments should not be used.

It should also be apparent that none of the diagnostic vocabulary activities deal with pronunciation or what is called "word recognition." Pronunciation assumes secondary importance to meaning recognition in content reading. Typically at stage 1 of Dale's rating scale (never heard of it) we cannot figure out the pronunciation of a word without assistance from an outside authority, be it teacher or pronunciation guide. Pronunciation of a term usually indicates that a student is a least at stage 2—having heard of the word. It seems apparent that going from a state of knowing what it means and how to use it requires time and effort. As with any topic in learning, an individual with more background information about a topic will have an easier time achieving mastery (Pearson, Hansen, & Gordon, 1979).

The next section deals with assessing reading comprehension from three viewpoints. Since goals should determine diagnostic instruments, two different situations are given.

Sample comprehension instruments

Situation: Seventh grade science class
Goals: To increase student knowledge of types of animals.
     To increase student interest in science.
    I. Skills approach
      A. Preview or survey reading
         Take five minutes to look through Chapter 3 (pp. 88-126). Then answer the following questions:
           1. How many major types of animals are described in this chapter?
           2. What are the names of the major types of animals?
           3. What points do scientists use to put animals into different classes? For instance, what points do scientists look at to put a snake into a different group from a dog?

4. Write down the numbers of each study question on page 107 that can be answered by reading just the subheadings.

B. Relating ideas

Read the section entitled Marsupials (pp. 109-113). Then use the words in the word box to complete the outline.

MARSUPIALS

Word Box
Attach to nipple. Where they live. Opossum will eat   almost any food. Crawl to pouch. What they eat.

1. Young are raised in a pouch in the mother's body.
   a. Born alive
      1.
      2.
      3.
   b. 1. Almost all live in Australian area.
      2. Opossums are only marsupial in the U.S.
   c. 1. Some marsupials eat only insects.
      2. Kangaroos eat only plants.

C. Main ideas

Reread the second paragraph on page 175 which begins with the words, "A marsupial is...." Decide which sentence below best states the main idea. Circle the number before the sentence you choose.

   1. Opossums live in the United States.
   2. Almost all marsupials live in or near Australia.
   3. The Tasmanian Devil is a marsupial.
   4. Kangaroos are the biggest marsupial.
   5. Marsupials live in a pouch after they are born.

D. Understanding graphics

Look at the diagram on page 121. Answer the following questions:

   1. This diagram is about _____.
   2. T F A pachyderm in an animal.
   3. T F A pachyderm is a mammal.
   4. T F A zebra is a pachyderm.

E. Recalling details
   From memory, list or pick from a list the names of three
   marsupials. _____, _____,
   _____.

   Name the only marsupial that lives in the United States.
   Name the largest marsupial. _____
   Give at least two reasons why the number of marsupials
   in the world has decreased.
F. Use and apply information you have learned about the
   ways marsupials a) are born, b) are cared for when
   young, c) eat, d) move from place to place, e) reproduce,
   f) adapt to their environment, and, g) defend themselves.
   List at least five ways a kangaroo is like a dog.
       They both _____
       _____
       _____
       _____
       _____

G. List at least three ways a kangaroo is like a person.
       They both _____
       _____
       _____

H. List at least three ways a kangaroo is different from a
   dog.
       A dog _____ but a kangaroo _____
       _____ _____
       _____ _____

I. If you found babies in the pouch of an opossum that had
   been killed by a car, what do you think the SPCA or the
   Natural History Museum would suggest you do to care
   for them? Specifically, what would they eat? What
   should you provide in their cage?

II. Introspective
   Implicit in the introspective questions is the fact that the
   students have been asked to survey the chapter and to make
   or complete an outline. This is *not* meant to imply that introspective instruments are tied to the previous skill instruments, but are used merely to provide continuity.
   1. List the things you looked at when you had five minutes
      to look over the whole chapter.
   2. Briefly explain how you completed the outline (note: this
      may be done orally in which case the teacher will keep
      brief notes).
   3. What did you do as you were reading to help yourself
      remember? (See note above.)
   4. Look back over the section on marsupials. If there were
      any parts which you did not understand, write the page
      number, paragraph, and first three words.

5. What did you do to try to make sense of the points you didn't understand?

Situation: Tenth grade social studies—Land Use in America in the 20th Century
Goals: Develop understanding of interrelations between people and nature.
Discover the range of variables to be considered in planning changes required by increasing population.
Formulate a general plan for making decisions about issues of land use.

III. Models
1. Cloze procedure
Simons lists the cloze procedure as a diagnostic test based on the theoretical principle of closure—the tendency for humans to complete what they see as incomplete. The cloze procedure consists of a portion of a text—generally about 300 words—in which every fifth word has been deleted and replaced with a blank. The student's task is to complete the passage.
Since cloze is based on student response to a text, it is also an appropriate measure of readability. Since both the procedure and related research are described by Pikulski and Tobin within this monograph no further description will be presented here.
2. Hypothesizing
Before reading or discussing the topic:
a. Pretend you are writing a chapter for a book entitled "Nature's Limits on Land Use." Write down three or more subtitles that you would include in the chapter.
b. Pick one of your subtitles and briefly explain why you would include it in the chapter.
3. Background knowledge
a. What land use decisions do you know of which have been in the news in the past three years?
b. Circle the number before any of the following issues which you have heard or read about.
1. (Love Canal) waste disposal dispute
2. (name) nuclear power plant protests
3. (name) shopping center dispute
4. (name) highway construction dispute
5. (name) housing project dispute
6. (name) water rights dispute
4. Strategy formation
a. Pretend that you are serving on a zoning board. You meet once a month. At every meeting you are

asked to make decisions about how to use land. Usually some people want a change and other people want no change. List the criteria (points you would consider) which you would use to make the decisions.

   b. Describe the steps you follow if you run across a point in your reading which you do not understand.

5. ReQuest procedure

   The ReQuest procedure (Manzo, 1973) is a task where students read a sentence or two and then exhange questions with the teacher. That is, each student has a chance to ask any question he/she chooses, then the teacher has a chance to ask questions. After several reciprocal sequences, students are asked to guess at the remaining content and read to check those guesses. Tape recordings of small group (5 to 8) ReQuest sessions will provide material to analyze reading ability and reading strategy in appropriate content material.

As in the case of vocabulary teaching, it is clear that students have a wider range of acceptable responses to the introspective and models questions. Therefore, diagnosis by introspective or models perspectives takes more time to evaluate. As any teacher knows, time is a most precious commodity. However, it is also possible to gather information about student progess as related to different goals through each of the three viewpoints. Therefore, the most efficient (in terms of time and information) means of gathering information about what students can do in relation to a teacher's goals depends not on the instrument but on the teacher goals.

Conclusions

In summary, informal evaluation of content reading is the act of discovering what a student can do in relation to a content teacher's instructional goals. Diagnosis is an intermediate step which logically falls between establishing clear goals and ongoing planning of classroom operations. Informal diagnosis of content reading ability may be viewed from the perspectives of readability, skills, introspection, or models of reading; but the instruments selected should provide information about each student in relation to the teacher's goals. With the approaches described above, diagnosis is not a one-time test, but may be carried out by careful evaluation of ongoing classroom activities. As long as teachers have clear goals and a measure of what a student can do, they are prepared to plan effective instruction.

References

Burmeister, Lou E. *Reading strategies for middle and secondary school teachers* (2nd ed.). Reading, Massachusetts; Addison-Wesley, 1978.

Dale, Edgar. *Vocabulary development.* Phi Delta Kappa Fastback, 1978.

Dale, E., & Chall, Jeanne S. A formula for predicting readability. *Educational Research Bulletin,* Ohio State University, 1948, *27,* 11-20.

Fredericksen, Carl H. Representing logical and semantic structure of knowledge acquired from discourse. *Cognitive Psychology,* 1975, *7,* 317-458.

Fry, E. A readability formula that saves time. *Journal of Reading,* 1968, *11,* 513-516.

Gray, W. S., & Leary, B. *What makes a book readable.* Chicago: University of Chicago Press, 1935.

Hansell, T. Stevenson. The effects of manipulation of syntax and vocabulary on reading comprehension. Unpublished doctoral dissertation, University of Virginia, 1974.

Hansell, T. Stevenson. Readability, syntactic transformations, and generative semantics. *Journal of Reading,* 1976a, *19,* 557-562.

Hansell, T. Stevenson. Increasing understanding in content reading. *Journal of Reading,* 1976b, *19,* 307-310.

Herber, H., & Riley, J. D. Research in reading in the content areas: A fourth report. Syracuse University Reading and Language Arts Center, 1979.

Kintsch, Walter, & Vipond, Douglas. Reading comprehension and readability in educational practice and psychological theory. In L. G. Nilsson (Ed.), *Memory: Processes and problems.* Hillsdale, New Jersey: Erlbaum, 1978.

Manzo, A. V. The ReQuest procedure. *Journal of Reading,* 1968, *13,* 123.

McGlaughlin, D. H. SMOG grading: A new readability formula. *Journal of Reading,* 1969, *12,* 639-646.

Pearson, P. D. The effect of background knowledge on young children's comprehension. Technical Report No. 116. Cambridge, Massachusetts: Bolt, Beranek and Newman, 1979.

Shepherd, D. L. *Comprehensive high school reading methods* (2nd ed.). Columbus, Ohio: Charles E. Merrill, 1978.

Simons, H. D. Comprehension: a new perspective. *Reading Research Quarterly,* 1971, *6,* 339-362.

Singer, H., & Ruddell, R. (Eds.). *Theoretical models and processes of reading* (2nd ed.). Newark, Delaware: International Reading Association, 1976.

Stein, N. L., & Nezworski, T. The effects of organizational and instructional set on story memory. Technical Report No. 68. Cambridge, Massachusetts: Bolt, Beranek and Newman, 1978.

Strang, Ruth. *Diagnostic teaching of reading.* New York: McGraw-Hill, 1964.

Thelen, Judith. *Improving reading in science.* Newark, Delaware: International Reading Association, 1976.

Winogard, Terry. Artificial intelligence: When will computers understand people? *Psychology Today,* 1974, *7,* 73-79.

Informal Approaches to Evaluating Children's Writing

Ronald L. Cramer
Oakland University

All of the other papers included in this volume address themselves to the evaluation of reading skills. One might ask why a paper is included which focuses upon the evaluation of writing. The basic reason is that writing and reading skills are highly related (Shanahan, 1980) and a substantial amount of professional opinion (Bush & Huebner, 1970; Combs, 1977; Durkin, 1976) as well as experimental evidence (Hunt, 1965; Stotsky, 1975; Zeman, 1969) suggests that the mental and language processes involved in written production of materials are the same or very similar to those involved in comprehending written materials. Thus, children's written compositions may mirror some of the skills or weaknesses that exist in reading comprehension and, therefore, offer one more avenue for making diagnostic judgments. This is not for a moment to say that the evaluation of writing is not a valued activity in itself. However, given the thrust and purpose of this volume it seems important to explicitly point out the well-documented relationship that exists between reading and writing.

The focus of the evaluation procedures discussed in this paper is to provide information about the teaching and learning processes implicit in writing. Three different and valuable approaches to the evaluation of writing skills will be discussed: teacher-evaluation, self-evaluation, and peer-evaluation.

Teacher-Evaluation: Holistic and Analytic Approaches

Holistic evaluation is a method of assessing writing to gain a global impression of its quality. In holistic evaluation each piece of writing is evaluated within two or three minutes. The evaluation is guided by criteria which specify what writing skills to consider; criteria are also developed which describe low, middle, and high levels of achievement in several skill areas related to writing. Such skill areas might include the quality of organization, the structure of sentences, and the use of correct punctuation. The purpose of holistic evaluation is to assess writing as a whole rather than to consider every detail. Consequently, writing deficiencies or strengths are not counted or quantitatively analyzed; general judgments are made and achievement is ranked on a holistic scale. For example, holistic evaluation of punctuation skills would not require counting the exact number of errors. Rather a decision would be made as to whether the punctuation merits a low, middle, or high ranking on a holistic scale designed to make holistic judgments possible. A holistic judgment regarding punctuation might be: 1) there are many punctuation errors—rank this piece *low* on punctuation; 2) there are a few punctuation errors—rank this piece of writing in the *middle* on punctuation; or 3) there are hardly any punctuation errors—rank this piece of writing *high* on punctuation. Rather than counting errors in punctuation, general guidelines such as the following are used to arrive at the ranking:

High. Consistently ends sentences with appropriate punctuation. Has strong control of internal punctuation and other less common punctuation. May experiment with punctuation marks not yet fully mastered.

Middle: Usually ends sentences with appropriate punctuation. Attempts to use internal punctuation, but makes some errors. Does not have control of the less common types of punctuation, but sometimes attempts to use them.

Low: Often fails to use ending punctuation correctly. Seldom uses internal punctuation. Less common punctuation is almost never used correctly. The final judgment is quickly recorded on a checklist of writing skills for holistic evaluation.

There are two dimensions along which written materials can be evaluated within a holistic evaluation framework: composing skills and mechanical skills. Because of the basic differences in style, content, and purpose of expository as compared to narrative materials, different aspects of composition skills need to be employed, depending on the nature of the writing. The charts shown are reproduced with permission from Scott, Foresman, 1981, and represent a summary of dimensions that can be used to evaluate narrative and expository writing holistically.

To facilitate the holistic evaluation of writing skills, it is recommended that teachers make copies of the charts shown, excluding the descriptions. Separate sheets could be prepared for expository materials or narrative materials. An abbreviated sample of an evaluation sheet is shown.

Evaluation Form for Narrative Writing

	(1) Low	**(2)** Middle	**(3)** High
STORY STRUCTURE			

It should be clear that children whose writing reflects good quality of organization of ideas will be likely to make use of the organization inherent in written materials that they read as an aid to comprehension. The child who uses good punctuation is very likely to be able to correctly interpret punctuation as an aid to reading comprehension. Essentially all of the qualities reflected in the standards listed have implications for better understanding the language and thinking processes common to reading and writing.

In contrast to holistic evaluation, analytic evaluation is a detailed counting and commenting on writing; and, unlike holistic evaluation, it is not dependent on general impressions, but on detailed analysis of each strength or weakness found in a piece of writing. The standards cited above can serve as the basis for such commenting so a dimension list will not be repeated here. In analytic evaluation, for example, punctuation, grammatical, and usage errors are corrected; other writing problems are noted and commented on in as much detail as seems necessary.

Undoubtedly, both analytic and holistic evaluation have utility. However, analytic evaluation is too time consuming to perform on every set of papers. Indeed, analytic evaluation of each piece of writing is impossible when children write frequently or when class size is large. The impossibility of analytic evaluation is obvious when the logistics are considered. For example, if an English teacher with 150 students spends ten minutes on each piece of writing, 25 hours would be required to evaluate one set of papers. How often can a teacher spend this amount of time analytically evaluating one set of papers? One solution is to use more efficient holistic procedures. A teacher skilled in the use of holistic procedures can reliably evaluate 150 papers in six hours or less. Once teachers have learned to use holistic evaluation they can assess a greater volume of writing than analytic procedures alone permit. Clearly, a balance between holistic and analytic evaluation is needed. A balanced allotment of time would be to evaluate about 75 percent of writing holistically and 25 percent analytically. This balance is expecially appropriate in classrooms where childen write frequently. Of course, not every piece of writing produced need be evaluated. There are legitimate writing assignments, such as certain types of journal writing, which require no teacher evaluation.

Self-Evaluation: Guidelines and Activities

Self-evaluation is the ability to improve one's own writing through self-directed editing and revision. It is the ability to look at a piece of writng holistically and conclude that it needs general improvement. It is the ability to look at a piece of writing analytically and locate the details that need correction or refinement. Self-evaluation is the ultimate writing skill. Careful, critical examination of one's initial impression or conclusion derived from what one reads may be the hallmark of a critical reader.

To edit or revise means to improve writing until it conforms to an acceptable standard of excellence. Standards of writing refer to the generally accepted writing conventions. These include technical matters such as grammar, usage, and mechanics as well as the more substantive writing skills, such as organization, paragraph structure, and wording. An acceptable standard of writing must be flexibly administered so that children's current writing ability and previous writing experience are taken into account.

Editing ability grows as children internalize the writing standards taught in the language program. When editing is taught in a variety of interesting and motivating ways, children develop the ability to examine their own writing critically. Writers should learn how to improve their own writing, even though some will never become outstanding self-editors.

Teaching editing is a challenging task. It is more difficult to teach children to evaluate their own writing than it is to evaluate for them. Teachers who have accepted the challenge have found that editing offers the best prospect for substantial writing growth. Of course, teacher evaluation must continue as part of the total evaluation program, but teachers must not waver from the ultimate goal: Teach children to be their own editors.

The following guidelines have been used by teachers who have succeeded in helping children to write freely and edit well.

1. *Using various activities to stimulate self-editing.* Editing activities should place children in various roles which require them to make judgments about their own writing and that of others.
2. *Modeling editing behavior.* The modeling of editing takes place when the teacher informally comments on children's writing, during conferences with children about their writing, and when teaching editing in whole class or group situations. It is essential to be sensitive, appreciative, and accurate in dealing with the personal writing of children.
3. *Encouraging children to listen to their own writing before editing it.* This may be done by working with a partner, by reading writing aloud, or by recording the writing and playing it back. Minor problems can be spotted immediately in this way, and, with experience, children will also learn to detect more serious writing problems.

There are many activities for stimulating editing. A few that have worked well in classrooms follow.

1. *Teaching editing regularly in editing workshops.* The editing workshop is a structured procedure for teaching editing skills. The procedures for teaching editing workshops are presented in detail under the discussion which follows on peer-evaluation.
2. *Having children write questions about the important ideas in their writing.* A partner reads the account and listens to the

question. The writer and the partner discuss any problems encountered. The discussion should lead to decisions about rewriting.

3. *Pairing a fifth or sixth grade class with a first or second grade class.* The older children act as editors and authors for the younger. After instructing the older children in the techniques of editing, have them help younger children with their writing. Young children often react more positively to an older child than to an adult.

4. *Instructing the children to underline certain words in their most recent writing.* They might, for example, be told to underline words that might be changed for more exact, vivid, or lively descriptions; or they might be directed to use a thesaurus or dictionary to aid in precise word selection.

5. *Placing editing charts in key places withing the room.* Children need help in learning to use specific elements listed in the charts to check their papers. The charts should cover two basic areas:

Composing Skills Chart
Did I say what I wanted to say clearly?
Did I choose the exact wording so others will understand?
Did I arrange paragraph details in logical or interesting ways?
Is each sentence well formed?
Does each paragraph have a main idea and supporting details?
Did I use more words than necessary?
Did my story have a clear beginning, middle, and ending?
Did I make the people and events real and interesting?

Mechanical Skills Chart
Does each sentence end with the correct punctuation?
Did I use punctuation in other appropriate places?
Did I capitalize the first word of each sentence?
Did I capitalize other appropriate words?
Did I spell words correctly and check words I was unsure of?
Did I write in my best handwriting?

These charts are general; more specific charts can be made to fit certain situations. However, editing charts are useless unless children have been taught how and when to use them.

A major responsibility in teaching writing is helping children to learn the skills of editing. Successful teaching of editing requires attention to detail, careful planning, and a general writing program that makes authorship an exciting enterprise without sacrificing discipline and responsibility.

Peer-Evaluation: Purpose and Use

When small groups of pupils work together to improve one another's writing, they are engaging in peer-evaluation. Peer-evaluation is a group editing experience intended to improve the writing of each individual child. It benefits the writing program in three ways:

1. Peer-evaluation improves writing, as research by Lagana (1972) and others has shown. Research in peer-evaluation shows that improvement has occurred in such areas as grammatical usage, organization, sentence revision, theme writing, and critical thinking. Interestingly, writing improvement brought about by peer-evaluation may be equal to or greater than improvement resulting solely from teacher evaluation.

2. Peer-evaluation helps pupils develop benchmarks against which to judge the quality of their own writing. Peer-evaluators are directed to look for the presence or absence of specific writing features in the writing of their peers. As pupils evaluate the writing of their peers they develop greater awareness of what makes their own writing understandable to others. Practice in applying writing skills in evaluation sessions helps pupils understand how these skills apply to their own writing and editing habits.

3. Peer-evaluation broadens the audience for each child's writing, thus giving an additional incentive for writing. Since pupils relate best to their peers, it seems reasonable that some writing should be evaluated by this natural audience. Broadening the audience for writing also stimulates children to select a wider range of topics and may encourage more sincere and forthright language expression.

Peer-evaluation has succeeded best where these three challenges have been squarely faced. First, pupils must be *taught* to evaluate writing sensitively and accurately. Second, pupils must be *shown* how to work together harmoniously in group settings. Third, teachers must be willing to *trust* pupils with the task of evaluating writing. When teachers face these challenges and are prepared to work hard to accomplish them, children's writing will improve.

Three steps are recommended for implementing a peer-evaluation program:

1. Teach the procedures for evaluating writing as a whole class activity prior to having pupils work independently in groups. Tell pupils they will be given a *Writing Workshop* for learning

how to evaluate their own writing and the writing of others. Follow these procedures:

a. Give a writing assignment on the day preceding the Writing Workshop. Have each pupil complete the writing assignment in first draft form.

b. Select one pupil's writing assignment (it is essential to secure permission and assure anonymity) and make a transparency. Project the draft material onto a screen. Tell the pupils to read the draft, then ask, "What are some things that have been done well in this draft?" List responses on the board. Initially, pupils often single out the mechanical technicalities of writing.

c. Tell the pupils to read the draft again. Then ask, "What are some things that should be changed to improve this draft?" Make the suggested changes on the transparency with a grease pencil and list them on the board.

d. Comment on each suggestion in a casual but informative manner. Comments should include information directly related to good writing practices as well as praise for thoughtful and accurate suggestions. No pupil's honest effort should go without acknowledgment.

e. Assign one or two items from the lists for pupils to evaluate in each other's drafts. For example, pupils may be assigned to work in pairs to look for sentence fragments in each other's drafts.

f. As the pupils work, circulate among them offering instruction and praise. For example, if a pupil cannot locate a sentence fragment, show the pupil where the problem is and explain how to recognize it as a fragment. Pupils will often discover strengths and weaknesses in each other's writing that they were not assigned to find. This behavior should be praised and rewarded. Other children will imitate this responsible behavior and some pupils will soon be doing a more thorough job. Of course, official responsibility is still limited to the specific task assigned for this particular writing workshop.

2. After pupils have gained evaluation experience through the writing workshop, they will be prepared for the more challenging peer-evaluation experiences described below:

a. After pupils have completed a writing assignment, organize them into groups of four to evaluate the paragraphs they have written. Have pupils use specific writing criteria, such as those shown below, to evaluate the paragraphs they have written.

Does the paragraph have a topic sentence that states the controlling idea?

Is the topic sentence at the beginning, middle, or the end of the paragraph?

Is each supporting detail related to the topic sentence?

Is the punctuation and capitalization in each sentence correct?

b. Have pupils make corrections and editorial comments on the paper each is evaluating. Explain that comments should be related to how well the evaluation criteria have been met for this particular paragraph writing assignment.

c. Have pupils rate the paper using a three point scale similar to the one given below. The rating system in the scale is as follows:

Low = 1 (The bottom 25 percent)
Middle = 2 (The middle 50 percent)
High = 3 (The top 25 percent)

First, familiarize pupils with the purposes and functions of a rating scale such as the one described. Once pupils understand how such a scale works, they will have little difficulty using it effectively.

d. Pupils exchange papers once again within their group. The second evaluator performs exactly the same functions described in steps b and c above. The purpose here is to have two different evaluations of each paper within the group.

e. Return the papers to the original writers for a rewrite and preparation of the final draft. Encourage pupils to discuss the editorial comments and ratings they have given.

f. After the final draft is prepared, reassemble the groups. Have pupils read each paper. Direct a discussion concerning the effectiveness of their evaluation work.

g. Have the pupils decide which of the four papers within their group best conforms to the criteria used to evaluate the work.

h. Collect the final drafts and assign final grades if you so desire. Of course, it is not necessary to the peer-evaluation process that this be done.

i. Since work that reaches the final draft stage often deserves a wider audience than it normally receives, the instructor may wish to have the class discuss ways in which this may be accomplished, such as through a class newspaper, bulletin boards, or even a Young Author's Conference.

3. The final stage of peer-evaluation involves groups of pupils jointly producing and editing special project writing assignments. For example, pupils may jointly write and edit a play, research report, story, or other work. However, this should not be attempted until the groups are working together harmoniously and effectively at the Step 2 level.

Peer-evaluation teaches children the basic skills of writing by having them edit and later produce written work within a group setting. The genuine audience that peer-evaluation provides is a powerful stimulus for learning. Implementing peer-evaluation requires considerable skill and dedication, but the rewards are often beyond the teacher's most optimistic expectations.

Conclusion and Summary

Evaluation is often thought of as a way to assess levels of achievement in writing in order to assign grades. Indeed, evaluation has this legitimate function. However, this paper has considered evaluation in a different light. Evaluation can also guide and inform teaching and learning. When children learn to revise their own writing and that of others, they acquire evaluation and writing skills simultaneously.

Teacher-evaluators can use holistic evaluation to gain quick impressions of writing. These impressions guide and inform group or individual writing instruction. Analytic evaluation achieves a similar purpose. However, analytic evaluation is more time-consuming than holistic evaluation. Thus, it is recommended that holistic evaluation be used more often than analytic.

Self-evaluation is a means of teaching children the skills usually exercised by the teacher. In the process of acquiring the evaluative skills required to revise their own writing, children improve their writing ability. Teachers need not feel guilty about transferring a share of evaluation responsibility to children. After all, revision is based on the premise that writers must learn how to evaluate their own writing if they are to become mature writers.

Peer-evaluation is an extension of self-evaluation. When children apply the skills they have gained in evaluating their own writing to the writing of their peers, they are merely extending the arena of opportunity for learning how to write.

Certainly the benefits of these informal evaluation procedures for the teaching of writing skills make them worthwhile in and of themselves. However, as cited earlier, there is also strong evidence to suggest that evaluation and improvement of writing skills will also have a positive influence on reading skills.

References

Bush, Clifford L. & Huebner, Mildred H. *Strategies of reading in the elementary school.* New York: Macmillan, 1970.

Combs, William. Sentence combining practice aids reading comprehension. *Journal of Reading,* 1977, *21,* 18-24.

Durkin, Dolores. *Teaching young children to read.* Boston: Allyn & Bacon, 1976.

Lagana, J. R. The development, implementation, and evaluation of a model for teaching composition which utilizes individualized learning and peer grouping. Unpublished doctoral dissertation, University of Pittsburgh, 1972.

Shanahan, Timothy. The impact of writing instruction on learning to read. *Reading World,* 1980, *19,* 357-368.

Standards for evaluating expository writing and standards for evaluating narrative writing. Reproduced with permission from Scott, Foresman. Materials taken from *Language structure and use,* 1981.

Stotsky, Susan. Sentence combining as a curricular activity: Its effect on written language development and reading comprehension. *Research in the Teaching of English,* 1975, *9,* 30-71.

Zeman, Samuel S. Reading comprehension and writing of second and third graders. *Reading Teacher,* 1969, *23,* 144-150.

Standards for Evaluating Composing Skills for Narrative Writing

	Low	Middle	High
STORY STRUCTURE	No identifiable beginning, middle, or end. Action and characters not developed or related. Essential details missing or confusing. Story problem not solved, or resolution unrelated to events.	Beginning, middle, and end present, but not always identifiable. Story problem presented, but not completely developed. Some conversational or descriptive details included. End may not show logical resolution of problem.	Identifiable beginning, middle, and end. Characters introduced and problem presented. Characters and problem well-developed with appropriate conversational or descriptive detail. Story ends with believable resolution of problem.
STORY SETTING	Setting of the story not identifiable. Details inappropriate and confusing.	Time and place of story are hinted at. But uncertain. Further references to setting may be inconsistent with original time or place.	Time and place of story clearly set. Specific details related to setting given in appropriate context. Setting consistent throughout.
STORY CHARACTERS	Characters not believable. Details related to character development are inconsistent, inappropriate, or missing. Difficult to distinguish one character from another. Action of characters unrelated to problem.	Characters somewhat believable. Some descriptive or conversational details given. Details may not develop character personality. Action of characters not always related to problem. Major and minor characters not clearly discernable.	Characters believable. Descriptive or conversational detail develops character personality. Action of characters relates to problem. Major characters more fully developed than minor ones.
STORY CONVERSATION	Conversation among characters haphazard, incomplete, or muddled. Much of the conversation inappropriate to circumstances and to personality of story characters. Conversation seems unrelated to story being told.	Conversation sometimes appropriate to circumstances and to characters. Conversation may reveal character personality or relationships among characters. Conversation sometimes not clearly related to story.	Conversation appropriate to story circumstances and to personality of each character. Conversation used to reveal character and develop interrelationships among characters. Conversation clearly relates to story.
STORY IDEA	Story idea is trite or otherwise uninteresting. Idea may lack freshness or imaginativeness. Story lacks plot or plot is vague. Story ends abruptly or reaches no definite conclusion.	Story idea is interesting. Idea may lack freshness or imaginativeness. Story has a plot. Plot may not be well-developed or entirely consistent. Story ending may not be satisfying or interesting.	Story idea is fresh or imaginative. Story plot is well-developed, is consistent, and comes to a satisfying, surprising, or otherwise highly effective ending.

Standards for Evaluating Composing Skills for Expository Writing

	Low	Middle	High
QUALITY OF IDEAS	Most ideas vague, incoherent, inaccurate, underdeveloped, or incomplete. Details often unrelated to topic. Nothing imaginative or thoughtful about the ideas.	Unevenness in completeness and development of ideas. Most ideas related to the topic; a few unrelated. Sound, but unimaginative ideas.	Ideas relevant to the topic, fully developed, rich in thought and imagination, and clearly presented.
QUALITY OF ORGANIZATION	Introduction, development, and conclusion unclear. Emphasis of major and minor points indistinguishable. Sentences and paragraphs seldom related by transitions. Overall lack of coherence and forward movement.	Introduction, development, or conclusion not easily identified. Emphasis on major or minor points sometimes not well-balanced. Transitions between sentences and paragraphs used, but without consistency. Forward movement variable.	Introduction, development, and conclusion well-structured, complete, and easily identified. Emphasis of major and minor points well-balanced. Sentences and paragraphs clearly related by transitions. Logical forward movement
SELECTION OF WORDS	Word selection inexact, immature, and limited. Figurative language seldom used.	Word selection usually suitable and accurate. Over-used words and clichés somewhat common. Figurative language may lack freshness, when used.	Facility and flair in word selection. Writer experiments with words in unusual and pleasing ways. Figurative language used, often in interesting and imaginative ways.
STRUCTURE OF SENTENCES	No variety in sentence structure; often only simple sentences are used. Transitions limited to such words as **then**; conjunctions limited to **and**. Awkward and puzzling sentences common. Run-on sentences and fragments often appear.	Some variety in sentence length and structure. Transitions used when necessary. Few sentence constructions awkward and puzzling. Run-on sentences and sentence fragments appear, but do not predominate.	Sentence length and structure varied. Sentences consistently well-formed. Smooth flow from sentence to sentence. Run-on sentences and sentence fragments rarely appear.
STRUCTURE OF PARAGRAPH	Topic sentences seldom used. Irrelevancies common. Order of details haphazard. Little or no command of the four common paragraph types.	Topic sentences usually stated. Irrelevancies uncommon. Order of details usually suitable. Limited ability to use the four common types of paragraphs.	Topic sentences stated and supported with relevant details. Appropriate variety used in ordering details (chronological, logical, spatial, climactic). Four types of paragraphs used when appropriate (narrative, explanatory, descriptive, persuasive).

Standards for Evaluating Mechanical Skills for Narrative or Expository Materials

GRAMMAR AND USAGE	Frequent errors in the use of nouns, pronouns, modifiers, and verbs.	Grammatical conventions of inflections, functions, modifiers, nouns, pronouns, and verbs usually observed. Grammatical errors sometimes occur.	Grammatical conventions of inflections, functions modifiers, nouns, pronouns, and verbs observed. Grammatical errors infrequent.
PUNCTUATION	End punctuation often used incorrectly. Internal punctuation seldom used. Uncommon punctuation is almost never used correctly.	Sentences usually end with appropriate punctuation. Internal punctuation used, with occasional errors. Uncommon punctuation sometimes used, but often inaccurately.	Sentences consistently end with appropriate punctuation. Internal punctuation and other less common punctuation usually correctly used.
CAPITAL-IZATION	First word of sentence often not capitalized. Pronoun/often a small letter. Proper nouns seldom capitalized. Other capitalization rules usually ignored.	First word of sentences nearly always capitalized. I always capitalized. Well-known proper nouns usually capitalized. Other capitalization rules used, but not consistently.	First word of a sentence and the pronoun/always capitalized. Well-known proper nouns nearly always capitalized. Good command of other capitalization rules regarding titles, languages, religions, and so on.
SPELLING	Frequent spelling errors. Shows a frustration spelling level (less than 70%). Unable to improve spelling accuracy in edited work without help. Misspellings often difficult to recognize as English words.	Majority of words spelled correctly. Shows an instructional spelling level (70 to 80%). Approaches 90% accuracy in edited work. Misspellings approximate correct spellings.	Nearly all words spelled correctly. Shows an independent spelling level (90%). Approaches 100% accuracy in edited work. Misspellings close to correct spellings.
HANDWRITING/ NEATNESS	Handwriting difficult or impossible to read. Letters and words crowded. Formation of letters inconsistent. Writing often illegible.	Handwriting usually readable, but some words and letters difficult to recognize. Some crowding of letters and words.	Handwriting clear, neat, and consistent. Forms all letters legibly with consistent spacing between letters and words.

The mechanical skills for writing are essentially the same for expository and narrative materials; therefore, only one chart is needed to describe the standards for evaluating either form of written work.

Informal Reading Inventories: A Critical Analysis

John J. Pikulski
University of Delaware
and
Timothy Shanahan
University of Illinois at Chicago Circle

Given the apparent widespread popularity of the informal reading inventory for reading evaluation, it seems appropriate to periodically critically evaluate the status of this major approach. In a 1974 publication, Pikulski attempted to comprehensively evaluate the available information about informal reading inventories and to make suggestions as to the directions that future research and inquiry might take. This paper is an attempt to look at the amount of progress that has been made toward answering some of the questions raised in that 1974 review, and to consider some new issues which have arisen.

There will be a focus on several research studies which help to answer questions about the reliability and validity of the procedures used for informal reading evaluation. Issues of interrater and alternate form reliability, criteria for establishing reading levels, differences between miscue analysis and informal reading inventory procedures, and the role of comprehension analysis are considered. Only tentative conclusions can be offered in many of these areas because of the limitations inherent in the available research.

An informal reading inventory consists of a sequential series of reading selections, graded in difficulty, which students read and answer questions about, and a set of procedures for analyzing the student's reading behavior in an instructional situation. The instrument used for this analysis can be a published inventory or it can be teacher constructed. Both forms of informal reading inventories will be discussed in this paper, and the reader is cautioned to keep the distinction between the two in mind.

Reliability

No serious treatment of formal assessment devices, such as a standardized group achievement test, would dare to omit a discussion of reliability if its authors expected the test to be accepted as a legitimate evaluation tool. However, it appears that many textbooks and published inventories ignore the issue of reliability when IRIs are the topic. This is unfortunate, as an assessment instrument certainly cannot be useful if the results it yields are unstable and affected by chance factors. Of course it could be argued that informal measures do not require the same level of reliability expected of formal tests because of the possibility of multiple administrations and ongoing observation of student behavior after the initial testing. For example, a teacher might employ an IRI to place a student in a reading book with an appropriate level of difficulty. Every time the student receives instruction in that book there is an additional opportunity to evaluate the accuracy of the initial test results. Although such continued monitoring could go a long way toward overcoming limitations in reliability, empirical data suggests that teachers do not make such alterations of instructional placements frequently (Austin & Morrison, 1961; Rosenbaum, 1980; Weinstein, 1976).

Even given ongoing evaluation, nothing is gained from the use of unreliable measures. The question of whether the results of informal reading inventories are consistent or reliable is still important. Unfortunately, a search of the literature reveals little that is new in helping us to answer that question in an informed way.

Interrater reliability. One form of consistency asks, will different examiners using the same instrument to measure the same thing get the same results? It's called interscorer or interrater reliability.

A 1975 study by Page and Carlson suggests that the results from informal evaluations may be far from consistent. They found that experienced reading specialists were not able to agree very consistently on the quality of oral reading. In their study, seventeen certified reading specialists listened to a tape-recorded oral reading performance. The teachers were directed to mark all miscues or errors, and to count them as they would in an informal reading inventory. They were to indicate whether the passage was at the student's independent, instructional, or frustration level. Although these teachers listened to the same tape, six rated the passage to be at the independent level, five said it was instructional, and six said frustration level.

Similarly, in a study by Allington (1978), teachers were found to be quite inaccurate in their analyses of a taped oral reading performance. No specific reliability data were reported in this study, but a large percentage of the teachers' errors appeared to be such that consistency is doubtful. The analyses of these 57 teachers differed markedly (on the average about 28 percent) from the number of errors actually on the tape.

However, studies by Lamberg (1975), Lamberg, Rodrigues, and Douglas (1978), and Roe and Aiken (1976), are more encouraging. Working with preservice teachers, they found that fairly good accuracy could be achieved, even over a relatively short period of time, if consistent, structured training techniques were used. Undergraduates were able to significantly decrease the number of errors they made in recording oral reading performance and were also able to improve in determining whether a deviation from the expected oral reading response was a reflection of the speech patterns of children from Spanish-speaking backgrounds.

The recency of the training appears to be an important factor in the consistency of evaluation which can be derived from an IRI. There appears to be a need for frequent posttraining checks to insure consistency of evaluation. The fact that the only studies in which consistent reading evaluations are found are studies in which all teachers take part in the same training program also suggests the strong possibility that reading personnel are exposed to a wide variety of training procedures which influence how they score and interpret informal reading inventories.

Alternate form reliability. A second form of reliability concerns whether one would get similar results even when two different forms of the same test are used. This reliability question would seem directly answerable for the published informal reading inventories, especially since most of them have several forms of the test at various grade levels. The Classroom Reading Inventory, for example, has three parallel sets of testing material (Forms A, B, and C) for each level, preprimer through eighth grade. Would one obtain the same results with form C or B as one would with A? Although the Classroom Reading Inventory is now in its third edition, the question of reliability is not addressed anywhere in the test materials. In general, it appears now, as it did in 1974, that some authors of published informal reading inventories do not feel a need to provide traditional psychometric evidence for the reliability or validity of these instruments.

The fairly recent Ekwall Reading Inventory is the only one of the published inventories available to us which directly addresses the subject of reliability. Ekwall (1979) reports a "preliminary study" involving 40 subjects. The study seems a study of alternate form reliability since Ekwall reports that the correlation between Forms A and C, which were used to measure oral reading performance, was .82 and the correlation between forms C and D was .79. However, Ekwall labels it a study of interscorer reliability because one examiner gave the tests in grades one through four and another gave the tests in grades five through nine. It still appears to us that it's a study of alternate form reliability. In any event the results are difficult, at best, to interpret since Ekwall doesn't even report what it was that was correlated. In addition, a reliability coefficient of only .79 is not particularly impressive since a frequently accepted guideline for an acceptable reliability coefficient for a test that is to be used for individual diagnosis is .90.

Several studies done in the past few years have also raised questions about the potential reliability for instructional material IRIs. In several studies, Bradley and Ames (1976, 1977) as well as Eberwein (1979), have presented evidence to suggest that basal readers vary considerably in readability. If a book designated as being at fourth reader level contains selections that range in readability from first to eighth grade level, then a child's reading performance at the fourth reader of a particular basal series may vary considerably depending on the passage the teacher or publisher selects to use in the informal reading inventory. This poses a serious threat to the whole concept of informal reading evaluation which suggests that the best way to tell whether children can successfully receive instruction in a given book is to ask them to read a small sample of that book. In their 1978 study, Bradley and Ames, after analyzing hundreds of passages selected from popular basal reader series, found that passages taken from a single level of a basal reader might vary in readability from first to twelfth grade level. In an earlier study, Bradley and Ames (1976) illustrated the effect that passage variability within the same basal reader book could have on oral reading performance. Students were found to be at a variety of levels of proficiency, although all of the IRI passages had been selected from a single basal reader.

In terms of variability of readability, at least some of the published inventories do present an advantage. Johns, for example, reports readability estimates for all of the passages used in the Basic Reading Inventory using both the Fry and either the Spache or Dale-Chall formulas. He presents the results for all levels and all forms of the inventory, and the results indicate that the readability is at or close to the designated levels of difficulty. Ekwall reports using the Harris-Jacobson formula to adjust the readability level of each passage to the midpoint of its designated level.

While the published inventories do seem to present information suggesting that passages are at their designated level of readability, comments such as that by Ekwall raise suspicions. Reviews of readability research (Klare, 1974-1975) suggest that readability formulae are reasonably good indices of difficulty of material and they warn that readability formulae were never intended as guides to the writing of materials. Simply shortening sentences and thus adjusting the readability designation of a passage, may have little or no effect on the actual level of difficulty of the passage (Hansell, 1976).

Error analysis. A frequent claim for informal evaluation is that it can yield valuable information about strengths and weaknesses that a person has in reading. It is not uncommon to

Pikulski and Shanahan

find that as a result of an informal reading inventory, a diagnostician concludes there are specific skills in word recognition or comprehension that a reader possesses and others that he or she lacks. Is there evidence that such analyses can be made reliably? No evidence concerning the reliability of such evaluations was found. Spache (1976, p. 141) criticized both commercial and teacher-made IRIs for the failure to "recognize that the number of errors analyzed should be 75-100 for a reliable diagnosis ... Repeated testing to obtain such a sample may be required to be certain that the remedial plan is formulated on a sound basis." This statement seems to cast doubt on the possibility of a reliable error analysis under typical circumstance, but Spache reaches this conclusion on the basis of studies of spelling accuracy and not studies of reading diagnosis (Spache, 1980). Spache's statement raises the need for caution in the analysis of reading errors or miscues. Future research should consider whether it is possible to derive a reliable assessment of specific skills through the use of traditional IRI methodology.

Validity and Criteria for Establishing Reading Levels

The question of validity—that is, does a test measure what it purports to measure—is difficult to address for any reading test, but again it is a central, critical concept for any assessment technique.

One validity issue surrounding reading inventories relates to the criteria recommended for establishing reading levels.

More than a decade ago, William Powell (1970) seriously challenged the traditional criteria for setting reading levels from informal reading inventories. The traditional criteria are usually attributed to Emmett Betts. Powell suggested that word recognition criteria be adjusted depending on the grade level of the child being evaluated informally. At first grade, for example, his research suggested that only 83 percent oral reading accuracy be required in order to establish an instructional level. The word recognition accuracy recommended for an instructional level rose successively at each grade level through sixth grade where 94 percent accuracy was required.

Unfortunately, little research has been done in an effort to determine the appropriate criteria for the establishment of levels since the review of informal assessment reported in 1974. Ekwall, Solis, and Solis (1973) reported a study of third, fourth, and fifth grade students who were given an informal reading inventory while they were monitored by a polygraph. Since polygraphs (often called lie detectors) are designed to measure anxiety, it was felt that through the use of the polygraph record the experimenters could discern the maximum amount of word recognition and comprehension errors a child could tolerate before stress and anxiety became apparent. Ekwall, Solis, and Solis failed to find any significant differences in reading scores associated with stress indicators that seemed related to the grade level of the child being tested, as would be predicted from Powell's position. Their data also suggested that the 90 percent word recognition criterion for a frustration level was associated with indicators of stress on the polygraph readings; this again challenges Powell's suggestion that 91 percent word recognition accuracy is adequate for an instructional level at third grade. This study, which is also reported in the *Reading Teacher* (1974) by Ekwall, and the *Journal of Learning Disabilities* (1976) by Davis and Ekwall, found that the amount of word recognition and comprehension errors that a reader can tolerate may also depend on level of intelligence, on whether the child is an achieving reader, and on some personality characteristics.

Since the available research seems limited, one might question professional opinion about IRI criteria for setting levels. In 1971, Powell and Dunkeld commented on the almost astonishing agreement of reading experts in accepting Betts' criteria in spite of the lack of experimental evidence to support those criteria. They found that among eleven authorities in the field only two proposed seriously different criteria, and one of these was Powell himself. We thought it might be interesting to see if the situation had changed over the nearly ten years since Powell and Dunkeld's report. We, therefore, selected from the shelves in our offices the first eleven reading texts we came across that had publication dates of 1978 or later and which discussed criteria for informal reading inventories. We were as surprised as Powell and Dunkeld had been with the agreement among reading professionals about the criteria to employ. Again, the vast majority of opinion suggests acceptance of Betts' criteria. Bond, Tinker, and Wasson (1979), Dallman, Rouch, Chang, and DeBoer (1978),

Durkin (1978), Farr and Roser (1979), Hall, Ribovich, and Ramig (1979), Ransom (1978), Roe, Stoodt, and Burns (1978), and Stauffer, Abrams, and Pikulski (1978), all recommend setting reading levels on the basis of the traditional criteria. Cheek and Cheek (1980), also accept Betts' criteria as an equally good alternative. They caution only that the diagnostician adopt one or the other set of criteria, indicating that evidence doesn't lead to a clear endorsement of either set. This was the only one of the eleven texts that did suggest that Powell's criteria were acceptable. Bader (1980) basically recommends the Betts criteria, with minor changes in the criteria for comprehension performance, but only in cases where silent reading precedes oral reading; otherwise, she recommends lower standards. Harris and Sipay (1978) suggest yet another set of criteria based on a 1952 study by Cooper, which compared scores on an IRI with the amount of reading test growth made over a year. Based on this study, Harris and Sipay recommend that the most suitable word recognition score for an instructional level in grades two and three is 99 percent, and word recognition scores of 97 to 99 percent for intermediate grades. The comprehension criteria recommended for an instructional level are 70 percent and up for second and third grades, and 60 percent and up for the intermediate grades. Interestingly, these criteria are more stringent at lower grades and less so at higher grades in direct contradiction to Powell's contention that children can tolerate the greatest degree of error at the lowest grades. It should be noted that Cooper's 1952 dissertation and Dunkeld's 1970 study are unusual in that they base their recommendations as to level setting criteria on the eventual progress students made in reading. Additional studies of this nature are needed.

Another place to look at professional opinion regarding criteria for informally establishing reading levels is in the published IRIs. Here, again, agreement is astonishingly consistent, and is most accepting of the traditional IRI criteria. The Classroom Reading Inventory, the Basic Reading Inventory, the Content Inventories, and the Diagnostic Reading Inventory all accept the traditional criteria; the Ekwall Reading Inventory also adopts the traditional criteria except that 60 percent or more comprehension is acceptable as an instructional level rather than the traditional 75 percent or more score. The Sucher-Allred

Reading Placement Inventory is the only published inventory that departs somewhat from traditional criteria. For an instructional level, the criteria are 92 to 96 percent accuracy for word recognition and are 60 to 79 percent for comprehension. Scores below an instructional level are at a frustration level; scores above the instructional level are acceptable for an independent level.

The agreement with respect to criteria among authors of published reading inventories is truly impressive—rarely do we see five out of six of our colleagues in essential agreement about anything. The agreement is even more impressive when we find that in addition to the strong agreement on the criteria for percentage scores, there is also widespread agreement on what constitutes an error. All of the inventories, with the exception of the Basic Reading Inventory, agree that omissions, insertions, substitutions, mispronunciations, and repetitions constitute errors. The Basic Reading Inventory departs seriously from the other published inventories by not counting repetitions as errors and by encouraging the examiner to count only "significant miscues." After examiners count the total number of miscues, they are directed to count the number of dialect miscues, all corrected miscues, and all miscues that do not change meaning. These "insignificant" miscues are not to be used for level setting. Johns' recommendation reflects the fact that there is an inescapable problem in weighing all errors equally. It was pointed out in the 1974 review that it is unquestionable that there are gradations of gravity in the types of errors made. It does seem less serious when a child substitutes the word "fruit" for "apple" as compared with not being able to attempt to pronounce the word. However, it would seem on the surface that the procedure advocated by Johns would yield substantially higher scores than would the procedure advocated by any of the other published inventories; yet Johns continues to advocate use of the traditional criteria scores for establishing reading levels. We see this as a potential problem since the traditional criteria were meant to apply to the oral reading accuracy scores based on all errors. Hoffman (1980), in an article which cautions against weighing the errors in informal reading inventories according to miscue analysis procedures, came to a conclusion which seems to warrant careful consideration. He writes: "There is no question that qualitative techniques of assessment such as miscue analysis are a far richer source of information for the discerning teacher than simple error counts. Qualitative techniques are revealing of ways in which instruction might be adapted to meet specific students' needs. It would appear advisable, however, that until such time as we are able to demonstrate how qualitative analysis can better meet demands for accurate placement of students in instructional materials than simple quantitative analysis, we should try to keep the two procedures as separate and distinct as the purposes for which they are used" (p. 138). In addition, we wonder if there might not be interscorer reliability problems stemming from differences in judgment as to what is and is not a "significant miscue."

It seems appropriate for all those who might consider changing basic IRI procedures to conduct some research on the effect that the changes might have in raising or lowering scores and to then consider establishing criteria. For example, Ekwall (1974) has suggested that repetitions not be counted as errors, and Gonzalez and Elijah (1975) indicate that passages should be read silently before oral reading analysis occurs. These changes are not unreasonable, but they serve to raise scores and would possibly lead to over placement in reading materials. When authorities recommend changes in procedures, they need to also address whether criteria for level setting need to be revised.

Informal Reading Inventories and Miscue Analysis

The Basic Reading Inventory is certainly not alone in recommending a kind of psycholinguistic interpretation of informal reading inventory results. In fact, a frequent recommendation with regard to informal evaluation during the past decade called for a wedding of informal methodology with miscue analysis, especially with respect to the interpretation of oral reading performance. A frequently heard criticism of informal reading inventories is that they stress the quantitative rather than the qualitative aspects of an oral reading performance. As Weaver and Smith (1979, p. 103) put it; "The major problem . . . is that many versions of the IRI encourage teachers to look primarily at the quantity of a reader's errors rather than the quality. Such a procedure may lead teachers to underestimate children's reading strengths and/or to prescribe inappropriate skills lessons." Though advocates of informal evaluation usually urge that the nature and severity of the errors be taken into consideration, they are usually sketchy in their description of just how this qualitative analysis be undertaken. Miscue analysis, with its identified categories for analyzing oral reading errors, seemed to many to be a natural accompaniment to informal evaluation. The use of traditional IRI numerical criteria could allow for the setting of independent, instructional, and frustration levels while more careful diagnostic observations regarding reading strengths and weaknesses might take place through miscue analysis. As Williamson and Young (1974) put it, "The power of the diagnosis made by using the Informal Reading Inventory and the Reading Miscue Inventory is increased if the concepts from both these techniques are synthesized. The IRI is an informal procedure for determining error count, four reading levels. . . . The RMI focuses on the quality of a reader's errors."

One immediate obstacle to the marriage, however, appears to be the alleged impracticality of miscue analysis for classroom use. It is frequently estimated that administration of a reading miscue inventory following the guidelines offered by Goodman and Burke (1976) takes well over an hour. In response to this criticism, articles such as those by Bean (1979), Christie (1979), Siegel (1979), and Tortelli (1976), proposed simplified procedures which were designed to shorten the amount of time needed to make a systematic qualitative interpretation of an oral reading performance. Christie suggested a two-step procedure wherein oral reading deviations from the text were first analyzed for their graphic similarity to the original text, as to whether they were semantically acceptable and self-corrected. The second step called for a summarization of this information in terms of the predominant strategies the reader employed.

We were able to locate no information in the literature as to how widespread the systematic use of a miscue analysis of informal reading inventory results has become. Our very informal observation, based on discussions with teachers and reading specialists, is that users of informal evaluation largely continue to rely predominantly on an "eyeballing" of the oral reading notations and to base their judgments on these relatively unsystematic analyses.

There is another difficulty that has been unearthed that presents problems for merging informal and miscue analysis procedures, a problem that may, in fact, be a general one for miscue analysis. This stems from the fact that there is a growing body of information which strongly suggests that the types of oral reading errors or miscues that are made are dependent on the level of difficulty of the material that is being read. As a reader moves from material that is only mildly or moderately challenging to material that is difficult, the type of oral reading errors or miscues that are made change.

One very consistent finding is that as a reader goes from reading materials that are at an instructional level to materials that are at a frustration level, there is a change in the type of error made, with a strong tendency to make less use of meaning and context clues (Christenson, 1969; Kibby, 1979; Leslie & Osol, 1974; and Williamson & Young, 1974). For example, Kibby used RMI procedures for coding such deviations from text to terms of its grammatical acceptability, semantic acceptability, and whether the miscue was corrected on the basis of the interrelationship of these dimensions. The reader was classified as having a strength, a partial strength, or a weakness in grammatical relationships. Using a population of fourth, fifth, sixth, and seventh grade disabled readers, he found that 4 percent of the students demonstrated a strength in grammatical relationships when reading a passage from the Spache Diagnostic Reading Scales that was judged too difficult to meet the standards for being at an instructional level, but a full 74 percent demonstrated this strength when reading a passage where instructional criteria were met. Similarly, Leslie and Osol (1974) found a significant difference between the number of uncorrected errors that resulted in a loss of meaning, depending on whether the eighth grade students, who were subjects in this study, were reading instructional level material or material that was more difficult than instructional level. When they were reading materials with 95 to 99 percent accuracy, they were significantly more likely to correct errors that produced a loss of meaning than when they read materials with 90 to 94 percent accuracy. Similar findings were obtained by Williamson and Young (1974) using elementary grade subjects who were reading at fifth grade level. They had students read from both basal readers and science materials. A study by Negin, reported by Pearson (1978), suggested approximately a 15 to 30 percent drop-off in the use of context at the frustration level from that appearing at the instructional level. This study also indicates that students frequently are unable to read known words (i.e., words they could read in isolation) in the context of frustration level material.

There does seem to be a fair amount of evidence to suggest that the pattern of errors that students demonstrate and the oral reading strategies that they employ will change with the level of challenge that those materials present to the reader. The more difficult the material, the less likely readers are to employ meaning and context clues, and the less likely they are to correct errors that detract from the meaning of the passage being read.

The implications of these findings seem twofold for informal evaluation. 1) It would seem to be inappropriate to group together all miscues and errors. It seems necessary to analyze them according to whether they are or are not at a subject's instructional level (a procedure which indicates the need for both qualitative and quantitative analyses). 2) The practice of using difficult materials for oral reading evaluation seems questionable, at best. Thus, the advice of Goodman and Burke (1976, p. 20) that materials to be used for constructing a reading miscue inventory be "one grade level above that which is usually assigned in class" may be inappropriate. It seems likely that a difficult passage such as suggested by Goodman and Burke will limit the extent to which a reader can employ language and context clues and will force an overreliance on graphic clues.

In addition to these implications, this fairly recent research on the changes that occur in the pattern of oral reading errors or miscues also seems to provide some added support for the traditional criteria since in several of the studies, readers began to become inefficient and began reading mechanically, rather than for meaning, as their performance dropped below 95 percent accuracy in word recognition.

Comprehension Analysis and the Informal Reading Inventory

The role of comprehension evaluation in the IRI was discussed briefly in the previous review. The brevity of the treatment was due to a dearth of available inquiry into informal comprehension assessment at that time. We assumed that the explosion of comprehension research which has occurred over the past few years would have led to an increase in research efforts concerning informal evaluation. Our search of the literature failed to uncover much in this regard. We have chosen to discuss, if only briefly, what we have found on this topic not because this material is sufficient to answer the important question concerning comprehension evaluation, but because it raises some issues which require further attention.

Both commercially published and teacher-constructed IRIs usually employ five to ten questions per passage to evaluate reading comprehension. The questions serve to direct students to read for meaning, and performance on the questions is actually used to assist in level setting. Sometimes specific error analysis, by question type, is recommended. These questions are often designed according to published guidelines (Johnson & Kress, 1965; Valmont, 1972). Recent research on the efficacy of such guidelines for designing appropriate questions has implications for IRI construction.

Davis (1978), for example, examined the ability of questions created by secondary teachers to discriminate between good and poor readers and between levels of difficulty. She reports that "as a whole, the set of inventory questions operates appropriately by demonstrating expected differences among the subjects and the graded passages" (p. 15). She also reported, however, that the individual questions, especially vocabulary questions, did not have high discriminatory power in distinguishing good and poor readers. Because of the limitations in the design of individual questions, Davis recommends a rethinking of the practice of encouraging teachers to construct IRIs, though her criticisms are probably equally valid for commercially published IRIs.

More problematical are the findings of Greenlaw and Peterson (cited in Peterson, Greenlaw, & Tierney, 1978) who reported that teachers, using each of three popular sets of question-construction guidelines, arrived at very different sets of IRI questions. That is, none of the popular guidelines used in this study were sufficiently well-defined to result in the creation of identical question sets. The impact of such differences upon instructional placement was demonstrated in another study (Peterson, Greenlaw, & Tierney, 1978). Utilizing one IRI with three different sets of questions designed according to a single set of guidelines, the reading skills of 57 children, grades two through five, were evaluated. The correlation of the reading placements derived from the three sets of questions ranged from .78 to .83. Different questions, in other words, result in the attribution of different reading level designations.

Thus, question variability leads to the attribution of different reading levels for the same reading behavior. This presents a problem for informal reading inventory construction of both the teacher-made and commercial varieties. Investigation is needed to find out whether it is possible to specify question writing criteria which will allow maximum discriminability of questions and which will lead to a more consistent reading level designation.

Teacher Constructed vs. Informal Reading Inventories

Throughout this review we have, as pointed out in the introductory section, discussed two somewhat different forms of informal reading inventories. One form is that of teacher constructed informal reading tests and a second is published informal reading inventories. There is a serious question as to how these two types of IRIs compare. In our search of the literature for this review, we were unable to find a single study which addressed this issue; therefore, we felt it appropriate to undertake a study aimed at providing at least a preliminary answer as to how the two types of IRIs compare. We were also somewhat interested in how these two forms of evaluation compared with a widely used, more standardized type instrument, notably the reading section of the Wide Range Achievement Test (WRAT).

Subjects

The subjects of this study were 33 students who were evaluated as part of the diagnostic service of the Reading Center at the University of Delaware. They represented a wide range in terms of age and reading ability. The mean age was 9-11 with a range from 7-2 to 15-11; average grade placement was 3.9 with a range from first through ninth; reading instruction levels ranged from preprimer through sixth. While all subjects had been referred for diagnosis because of a suspected reading problem, eight or 24 percent of the subjects were diagnosed as having a reading level that was at their grade placement. (This is not to imply that they were reading at an appropriate level. While one might expect a child with above average intelligence to read above grade level, for purposes of this study it did not seem imperative to address this issue.) Thus, the study looks at students' reading both at or below grade placement. None of the students tested was reading above grade placement.

Test Materials

As part of a larger diagnostic battery, each subject in this study was given each of the following reading tests: The Reading Section of the Wide Range Achievement Test (Jastak & Jastak, 1978), the Basic Reading Inventory (Johns, 1978), and a clinician constructed informal reading inventory. To accomplish the last measure, students coming for the evaluation were requested to bring with them a copy of the reading text they were currently using in school. From this text, the clinician responsible for conducting the diagnosis of this youngster constructed an IRI following the directions provided in Stauffer, Abrams, and Pikulski (1978). All clinicians had received at least one month's training in the construction and administration of tests. All were Master's degree candidates working on a full time basis at the Reading Center. In addition, because of the questions raised previously in this chapter about the interpretation of the results of the Basic Reading Inventory, the procedures for recording, scoring, and calculating the results of that measure were the same employed with the teacher-constructed IRI.

Results

Because of the preliminary nature of the study, complex analyses of the data seemed inappropriate. Instead, the data were analyzed in a simple, straightforward fashion to answer the following questions:

1. How did the average grade level score for the teacher-constructed IRI, the published IRI, and the WRAT compare?

There was an outstanding amount of agreement between the two forms of IRI. The average grade score for the clinician constructed instrument was 1.88 while the average grade score for the published IRI was 1.70; both were approximately second grade level. In sharp contrast the average grade score on the Reading Section of the WRAT was 4.01 or fourth grade—more than two grade levels above the scores obtained from the IRIs.

2. How frequently would students be placed at the same instructional reading levels by the three measurement instruments and how frequently would the results vary by one grade level or more?

Here again the results of the two IRIs are remarkably consistent—22 of the total population of 33 (67 percent) students were placed at the same instructional level; the remaining 11 or 33 percent were within one grade level of each other. There was some tendency for the clinician constructed IRI to yield somewhat higher scores. Of the 11 students who were within one year of each other, eight (24 percent) of the total of 33 scored one grade level higher on the clinician constructed IRI; while only three (9 percent) of the total population scored one year higher on the published IRI than they did on the clinician constructed version. As one might expect from the average grade scores reported earlier, there was not nearly so close an agreement between the WRAT and the IRIs. When compared to the clinician constructed IRI, the two measures never placed students at the same grade level. The WRAT score was one grade lower for one child or 3 percent of the population. By far the outstanding tendency was for the WRAT to yield much higher scores. It placed 12 (37 percent) of the students one grade level higher than did the clinician constructed IRI; 10 students (30 percent) were placed three levels higher on the WRAT than on the clinician constructed IRI.

The results obtained when comparing the instructional levels for the WRAT and the published IRI were remarkably similar to those just discussed; therefore, these results will not be reported in order to conserve space.

Discussion

The authors of this chapter were extremely surprised by the high degree of agreement between the two types of IRIs. Based upon clincial observations of test data, we had anticipated far less agreement. The results were thus extremely encouraging.

It should be pointed out that these results were obtained using the same recording, scoring, and interpretation procedures with both the clinician constructed and published IRIs and that the measures were administered by the same clinician. All levels were set only after review by the faculty supervisor of the Diagnostic Service. It seems almost certain that if the procedures outlined by the author of the published IRI had been followed, substantially less agreement would have been achieved. Thus, these results largely suggest that if similarly trained clinicians use agreed upon procedures and criteria, they can obtain very similar results with respect to setting an instructional level regardless of whether they construct their own IRI or use published materials.

As indicated previously, we had not anticipated so close an agreement. One possible reason for this is that at times the differences obtained in an actual reading performance were dramatic, even though the same instructional level was established using both IRIs. For example, in one case a second grade child who scored below a preprimer instructional level achieved an oral reading accuracy score of 92 percent when reading an IRI selection based upon the preprimer instructional materials being used in school; the 92 percent score also represented a rather labored oral reading and, therefore, the child was judged to fall below standards even at a preprimer level. However, when asked to read the preprimer passage from the published reading inventory, this child achieved an oral reading score of only 32 percent. Though the instructional level was still below the preprimer, the two oral reading performances were dramatically different. Visual inspection of the actual scores from the two IRIs suggested that children who were reading at a first reader level or below were more likely to do better on an informal reading inventory based on their instructional materials than on some general, published IRI. Given the fact that instructional materials vary considerably in the vocabulary and skills that they introduce, especially in the earliest levels of the programs, this is hardly a surprising finding. It does suggest, however, that the use of a general, published IRI with beginning readers may not reflect the specific vocabulary and skills that they have mastered in their program of reading instruction. It may, on the other hand, give a good estimation of the general or functional reading skills mastered by the student.

The results of this preliminary study confirm the impressions of many reading specialists that the reading section of the WRAT seriously overestimates a child's instructional level. While the WRAT may have utility as a quick, gross screening device, these results suggest that approximately one out of three times it will overestimate a child's instructional level by as much as three grade levels.

One final observation seems in order. There was a substantial amount of agreement between teacher judgment as reflected in the book placement of the subject tested and the results of both IRIs. For example, when the instructional level from the clinician constructed IRI was compared with the level at which the child was actually receiving instruction, the grade level was the same for 21 (64 percent) of the 33 subjects. Three (9 percent) children were underplaced, that is their instructional level established by the IRI was a year higher than the level of the book in which they were receiving instruction. Nine of the children (27 percent) were overplaced according to these results. Seven of them (21 percent) were placed in books above the instructional level established by our testing, and two (6 percent) were in books two levels above their established instructional level. Given the fact that there is likely to be some degree of error in our measurement, and the difficulties involved in interpreting reading test results, teacher judgment for this group of youngsters appears to be accurate to an encouraging degree.

Summary and Conclusions

Based on the review that has just been made, the following conclusions seem in order with respect to the use and interpretation of the IRI.

1. Published IRIs in particular should provide information about alternate form and test-retest reliability. Research is needed to indicate the reliability of judgments

Pikulski and Shanahan

regarding specific skill strengths and weaknesses derived from an IRI performance.

2. Because a given reading text may contain selections which vary considerably in readability, teachers and other diagnosticians should carefully choose selections when constructing an informal reading inventory. When using an IRI that was constructed by a publisher to accompany its reading materials, users should critically ask if it is similar in content and skill demands to the materials that are being considered for use with the child being tested.

3. Though the empirical support for the use of the traditional criteria for establishing independent, instructional, and frustration levels is exceedingly weak, professional opinion is very supportive of their acceptance. Until more complete, more convincing, and more consistent research results suggest adoption of some other set of criteria, it seems best to employ those generally attributed to Betts.

4. Errors or miscues should be analyzed both *qualitatively* and *quantitatively*. Miscue analysis or some simplified adaptation of it seems a reasonable framework for a qualitative analysis.

5. The qualitative analysis of oral reading errors or miscues should focus on the deviations from text that take place at or very near a child's instructional level if these are to be used to make recommendations for instruction.

6. Until more research results are available, it seems unwise to calculate accuracy of an oral reading score that takes into account the psycholinguistic properties of the miscue or error. It would seem that new criteria for reading levels would need to be developed based on such an analysis. Calculating the accuracy of an oral reading score based on the psycholinguistic properties of the error would seem to alter the traditional criteria in an unknown fashion. The same can be said of any major changes in basic IRI procedures which lead to alterations of student performance levels; such changes would seem

likely to require similar adjustments in the traditional criteria.

7. More studies are needed which attempt to establish the validity of informal evaluation and the criteria that should be used in establishing levels by determining how well IRI results predict the amount of progress that children make in reading.

8. Future efforts need to be directed towards the design of question writing guidelines which will allow the creation of more discriminable questions which result in a stable attribution of reading levels.

There are many questions that remain unanswered and issues that remain unresolved with respect to the use of the informal reading inventory. It seems likely that this will not diminish the popularity of the approach since many, perhaps most, of those issues are not unique to informal reading inventories, but are shared by other approaches to reading evaluation. The strength of the IRI very likely lies in the close match that it can allow between testing and teaching. Because we see this as the central characteristic of IRIs, we also see a guiding principle for how to decide on the details of administering, scoring, and interpreting IRIs—do things the way you would do them when teaching reading.

References

Allington, Richard L. Teacher ability in recording oral reading performance. *Academic Therapy,* 1978, *14,* 187-192.

Austin, Mary C., & Morrison, Coleman. *The first r: The Harvard report on reading in elementary schools.* New York: Macmillan, 1963.

Bader, Lois A. *Reading diagnosis and remediation in classroom and clinic.* New York: Macmillan, 1980.

Bean, Thomas W. The miscue miniform: Refining the informal reading inventory. *Reading World,* 1979, *18,* 400-405.

Bond, Guy L., Tinker, Miles A. & Wasson, Barbara B. *Reading difficulties, their diagnosis and correction* (4th ed.). Englewood Cliffs, New Jersey: Prentice-Hall, 1979.

Bradley, John M., & Ames, Wilbur S. The influence of intrabook readability variation on oral reading performance. *Journal of Educational Research,* 1976, *70,* 101-105.

Bradley, John M., & Ames, Wilbur S. Readability parameters of basal readers. *Journal of Reading Behavior,* 1977, *9,* 175-183.

Cheek, Earl H., and Cheek, Martha. *Diagnostic-prescriptive reading instruction.* Dubuque, Iowa: Wm. C. Brown, 1980.

Cooper, J. Louis. The effect of adjustment of basal reading materials on achievement. Unpublished doctoral dissertation, Boston University, 1952.

Christie, James F. The qualitative analysis system: Updating the IRI. *Reading World,* 1979, *18,* 393-399.

Christenson, Adolph. Oral reading errors of intermediate grade children at their independent, instructional, and frustration levels. In J. Allen Figurel (Ed.) *Reading and realism.* Newark, Delaware: International Reading Association, 1969, 674-677.

Dallman, Martha, et al. *The teaching of reading* (4th ed.) New York: Holt, Rinehart, and Winston, 1978.

Davis, Carol. The effectiveness of informal assessment questions constructed by secondary teachers. In P. David Pearson and Jane Hansen (Eds.), *Reading: Disciplined inquiry in process and practice,* Twenty-Seventh Yearbook of National Reading Conference. Clemson, South Carolina: National Reading Conference, 1978, 13-15.

Davis, Everett E., & Ekwall, Eldon E. Mode of perception and frustration in reading. *Journal of Learning Disabilities,* 1976, *9,* 53-59.

Dunkeld, Colin G. The Validity of the informal reading inventory for the designation of instructional reading levels: A study of the relationships between children's gains in reading achievement and the difficulty of instructional materials. Unpublished doctoral dissertation, University of Illinois, 1970.

Durkin, Dolores. *Teaching them to read* (3rd ed.) Boston: Allyn and Bacon, 1978.

Eberwein, Lowell D. The variability of readability of basal reader textbooks and how much teachers know about it. *Reading World,* 1979, *18,* 259-272.

Ekwall, Eldon E. *The Ekwall reading inventory.* Boston: Allyn and Bacon, 1979.

Ekwall, Eldon E. Should repetitions be counted as errors? *Reading Teacher,* 1974, *27,* 365-367.

Ekwall, Eldon E., Solis, Judy K., & Solis, Enrique. Investigating informal reading inventory scoring criteria. *Elementary English,* 1973, *50,* 271-274, 323.

Farr, Roger, & Roser, Nancy. *Teaching a child to read.* New York: Harcourt Brace Jovanovich, 1979.

Gonzalez, Phillip C., & Elijah, David V. Rereading: Effect on error patterns and performance levels on the IRI. *Reading Teacher,* 1975, *28,* 647-652.

Goodman, Yetta M., & Burke, Carolyn L. *Reading miscue inventory.* New York: Macmillan, 1972.

Hall, MaryAnne, Ribovich, Jerilyn K., & Ramig, Christopher J. *Reading and the elementary school child* (2nd ed.). New York: D. Von Nostrand, 1979.

Hansell, T. Stevenson. Readability, syntactic transformations, and generative semantics. *Journal of Reading,* 1976, *19,* 557-562.

Harris, Albert J., & Sipay, Edward R. *How to increase reading ability* (6th ed.). New York: David McKay, 1975.

Hoffman, James V. Weighting miscues in informal inventories—a precautionary note. *Reading Horizons,* 1980, *20,* 135-139.

Jacobs, H. Donald, & Searfoss, Lyndon W. *Diagnostic reading inventory.* Dubuque, Iowa: Kendall/Hunt, 1977.

Jastak, Joseph F., & Jastak, Sarah R. *Wide range achievement test.* Wilmington, Delaware: Jastak Associates, 1978.

Johns, Jerry L. *Basic reading inventory.* Dubuque, Iowa: Kendall/Hunt, 1978.

Johnson, Marjorie Seddon, & Kress, Roy A. *Informal reading inventories.* Newark, Delaware: International Reading Association, 1965.

Kibby, Michael W. Passage readability affects the oral reading strategies of disabled readers. *Reading Teacher,* 1979, *32,* 390-396.

Klare, George R. Assessing readability. *Reading Research Quarterly,* 1974-1975, *10,* 62-102.

Lamberg, Walter J. Accuracy in measuring oral reading in English by a student with a Spanish language background. ED 128 767, 1975.

Lamberg, Walter J., Rodriguez, Laura, & Tomas, Douglas. Training in identifying oral reading departures from text which can be explained as Spanish-English phonological differences. Paper presented at the annual meeting of the Southwest Educational Research Association, Austin, Texas, 1978.

Leslie, Lauren, & Osol, Pat. Changes in oral reading strategies as a function of quatities of miscue. *Journal of Reading Behavior,* 1978, *10,* 442-444.

McWilliams, Lana, & Rakes, Thomas. *Content inventories: English, social studies, science.* Dubuque, Iowa: Kendall/Hunt, 1979.

Page, William D., & Carlson, Kenneth L. The process of observing oral reading scores. *Reading Horizons,* 1975, *15,* 147-150.

Pearson, P. David. On bridging gaps and spanning chasms. *Curriculum Inquiry,* 1978, *8,* 353-363.

Peterson, Joe, Greenlaw, M. Jean, & Tierney, Robert J. Assessing instructional placement with the IRI, the effectiveness of comprehension question. *Journal of Educational Research,* 1978, *71,* 247-250.

Pikulski, John J. A critical review: Informal reading inventories. *Reading Teacher,* 1974, *28,* 141-151.

Powell, William R. Reappraising the criteria for interpreting informal inventories. In Dorothy L. DeBoer (Ed.), *Reading diagnosis and evaluation.* Newark, Delaware: International Reading Association, 1970, 100-109.

Powell, William R., & Dunkeld, Colin G. Validity of the IRI Reading Levels. *Elementary English,* 1971, *48,* 637-642.

Ransom, Grayce A. *Preparing to teach reading.* Boston: Little, Brown, 1978.

Roe, Betty D., Stoodt, Barbara D., & Burns, Paul C. *Reading instruction in the secondary school.* Chicago: Rand McNally, 1978.

Roe, Michael, & Aiken, Robert. A CAI simulation program for teaching IRI techniques. *Journal of Computer Based Instruction,* 1976, *2,* 52-56.

Rosenbaum, James E. Social implications of educational grouping. In David C. Berliner (Ed.), *Review of research in education,* Volume 8, American Educational Research Association, 1980, 361-401.

Siegel, Florence. Adapted miscue analysis. *Reading World,* 1979, *19,* 36-43.

Silvaroli, Nicholas J. *Classroom reading inventory,* Boston: Allyn and Bacon, 1979.

Spache, George D. *Diagnosing and correcting reading disabilities.* Boston: Allyn and Bacon, 1976.

Spache, George D. Personal correspondence, July 25, 1980.

Stauffer, Russell G., Abrams, Jules C., & Pikulski, John J. *Diagnosis, correction, and prevention of reading disabilities.* New York: Harper and Row, 1978.

Sucher, Floyd, & Allred, Ruel. *Sucher-Allred reading placement inventory.* Provo, Utah: Brigham Young University Press, 1968-1971.

Tortelli, James P. Simplified psycholinguistic diagnosis. *Reading Teacher,* April 1976, 637-639.

Valmont, William J. Creating questions for informal reading inventories. *Reading Teacher,* 1972, *25,* 509-512.

Weaver, C., & Smith, L. A. Psycholinguistic look at the informal reading inventory: Part 2—Inappropriate inferences from an informal reading inventory. *Reading Horizons,* 1979, *19,* 2, 103-111.

Weinstein, Rhona S. Reading group membership in first grade: Behaviors and pupil experience over time. *Journal of Educational Psychology,* 1976, *68,* 103-116.

Williamson, Leon E., & Young, Freda. The IRI and RMI diagnostic concepts should be synthesized. *Journal of Reading Behavior,* 1974, *6,* 183-194.

A PUBLISHING PROGRAM
TO SERVE YOUR NEEDS...

The development of professional publications that uniquely meet the current needs and expectations of reading teachers, researchers, librarians, and other educators is a major goal of the International Reading Association. Your brief responses to the questions below will help us plan for the future.

Approaches to the Informal Evaluation
of Reading   John Pikulski and Timothy Shanahan, Editors

This book came to my attention through
- _____ my membership in IRA
- _____ my school library
- _____ a colleague
- _____ my child's interests in reading
- _____ other (*please specify:* _____)

Chapters which interested me most were

_____   _____

_____   _____

Least helpful portions of the book were

_____   _____

_____   _____

Topics that I wanted to know more about were

_____   _____

_____   _____

My needs would best be served through
- _____ interpretations of research
- _____ practical suggestions for classroom use
- _____ help for parents
- _____ other (*please specify:* _____)

Use reverse side for additional comments and free samples.

Reactions to this volume...(*continued*)

Especially for nonmembers

Fill in this form if you are not presently a member and are interested in more information about the International Reading Association.

Name _____ Professional affiliation _____

Address _____ _____

_____ Areas of special interest _____

_____ _____

Please send me the following free items:

A Sample IRA journal _____ (Elementary)

_____ (Secondary)

_____ (Research in reading)

_____ (Spanish language)

_____ Current *IRA Publications Catalog* of titles and prices

_____ Sample copy of *Reading Today*, IRA's newsletter to members

_____ *Studying: A Key To Success...Ways Parents Can Help*

Check for FREE SAMPLES!

Forward your comments to
IRA PROFESSIONAL PUBLICATIONS
P.O. Box 8139
Newark, Delaware 19711